*Time, Form, and Style in
Boswell's Life of Johnson*

TIME, FORM,
AND STYLE IN

Boswell's
Life of
Johnson

BY DAVID L. PASSLER

NEW HAVEN AND LONDON
YALE UNIVERSITY PRESS
1971

Designed by Sally Sullivan
and set in Linotype Baskerville type.
Printed in the United States of America by
The Carl Purington Rollins Printing-Office
of the Yale University Press.

Distributed in Great Britain, Europe, and Africa by
Yale University Press, Ltd., London; in Canada by
McGill-Queen's University Press, Montreal; in Mexico
by Centro Interamericano de Libros Académicos,
Mexico City; in Central and South America by Kaiman
& Polon, Inc., New York City; in Australasia by
Australia and New Zealand Book Co., Pty., Ltd.,
Artarmon, New South Wales; in India by UBS Publishers'
Distributors Pvt., Ltd., Delhi; in Japan by John
Weatherhill, Inc., Tokyo.

For Albrecht Strauss

CONTENTS

ACKNOWLEDGMENTS

Making a list of all the people who have aided one with a project inevitably entails the risk of categorizing friends and kind colleagues and of suggesting an overly neat view of the progress of one's work. I hope that those who are used to reading such debts of gratitude will be able to see behind this short account the variety of helpful letters, conversations, and last-minute favors that gradually propel a book toward its completion despite the relative clutter in which most of us think and live.

My prime debt is to Albrecht Strauss, whose graduate course in the Age of Johnson was my introduction to the eighteenth century. He supervised several years ago the growth of this study in its first form, as a dissertation, and has helped me often during my period of rethinking and rewriting.

I am extremely grateful for the pleasant, productive time that I spent with the Boswelliana at the Beinecke Rare Book and Manuscript Library. The success of my stay there was ensured by the expansive kindness of Herman W. Liebert and especially Marion Pottle, who was always eager to help me decipher Boswell's handwriting or locate a relevant document.

Certain passages of this study owe their present form to

specific conversations I had with Dougald MacMillan, Harry Berger, Jr., Frederick Pottle, William K. Wimsatt, Jr., and Jerome Beaty.

Both Professor Pottle and J. Paul Hunter have read the manuscript and suggested improvements in style, argument, and content.

Alice Bliss ably typed the manuscript in its final form.

My most recent debt is to the editors at the Yale Press who have worked with me: Wayland Schmitt, Ellen Graham, and Cynthia Brodhead.

D. L. P.

INTRODUCTION

This study views Boswell's *Life of Samuel Johnson* as literature, that is, as an imaginatively coherent work with certain cooperating devices of narration and verbal style. Furthermore, Boswell's portrait is vivid, moving, and unforgettable both because of this coherence and because of the ways in which it is threatened by unassimilable historical facts. Boswell's literary craftsmanship too long escaped examination because the excellence of the *Life* clearly seemed to depend on Johnson's enormous importance as a man of letters, an ethical ideal, and a culture hero of the middle class.

Early comments on the *Life* itself usually concentrated on possible literary models, such as the character sketches of Xenophon and Suetonius and the biographical compilations of Thomas Fuller, Gerard Langbaine, and Anthony à Wood. Although these works catered to Boswell's love of anecdotes, they did not directly influence his style or even his format, since they were for him primarily a medicine to purge melancholy: "I look upon the *Biographia Britannica* with that kind of grateful regard with which one who has been recovered from painful indisposition by their medicinal springs beholds Bath, Bristol, or Tunbridge."[1] Saints' lives were obvious models for writing the life of a great man, and

1. *The Hypochondriack*, ed. Margery Bailey, 1: 149.

Walton's rather idealistic and oversimplified *Lives* combine
the hagiographical tradition with the Theophrastian-Over-
burean character. Walton's intermittent use of personal letters was expanded in Middleton's *Life and Letters of Marcus
Tullius Cicero* (1741) and Mason's *Life of Gray* (1775). The
latter was one of Boswell's avowed models, though a comparison of Mason's biography with the *Life of Johnson*
reveals the casualness of his claim; the letters in the *Life of
Gray* are large blocks rather awkwardly cemented together
by Mason's contributions, none of which resembles the Boswellian conversations. Although Johnson's *Life of Savage*
(1744) and *Lives of the Poets* (1779–81) were Boswell's most
immediate models, he followed them only in part: he, like
Johnson, worked to expose the vices as well as the virtues of
his subjects, but most of the Johnsonian essays have the
tripartite structure of life, literary criticism, and character
sketch.

Thus, when Boswell began the *Life,* eighteenth-century
biography consisted of four types, each seldom occurring in
a pure state: anecdote, chronicle, moral tale, and compilation
of sayings, letters, and excerpts from works. Boswell was able
to combine these types with his recorded conversations to
create a biography of unparalleled immediacy and breadth.[2]
But left unexplained is the uniqueness of Boswell and the
Life. Significantly, his personality and his craftsmanship have
been inseparable for most readers. During his lifetime there
were those like Peter Pindar who considered him a Lazarus
gathering scraps at a rich man's table, and this view held
increasing sway after the death of the last of his contempo-

2. Boswell's antecedents and innovations are described by Donald A.
Stauffer in *English Biography before 1700* and *The Art of Biography in
Eighteenth-Century England.* More recent attempts to find Boswell's
models in the drama have so far been convincing for only short sections
of the *Life:* see Sven Eric Molin, "Boswell's Account of the Johnson-
Wilkes Meeting."

raries. The problem of Boswell's personality became the problem of explaining the apparent disjunction between the sustained high quality of the *Life* and the shortcomings of its author.

Macaulay tried to solve the problem by resorting to the "paradox" of Boswell's temperament. His explanation is a classic example of how an apparent paradox is often the result of rhetoric swamping insight.

> He had, indeed, a quick observation and a retentive memory. These qualities, if he had been a man of sense and virtue, would scarcely of themselves have sufficed to make him conspicuous; but, because he was a dunce, a parasite, and a coxcomb, they have made him immortal.[3]

Macaulay was actually reviewing Croker's grotesque conflation of the *Life* with the relevant passages from Mrs. Piozzi, Garrick, Goldsmith, Hawkins, and the *Tour to the Hebrides*, but this notion of the Boswellian paradox, as vivid as it was distorted, caught the popular imagination and led to other scissors-and-paste treatments that at least tacitly denigrated Boswell's artistry. This long tradition includes E. T. Mason's *Samuel Johnson: His Words and His Ways. What He Said, What He Did, And What Men Spoke Concerning Him* (New York, 1879), James Hay's *Johnson: His Characteristics and Aphorisms* (London, 1884), and Raymond Postgate's *The Conversations of Dr. Johnson* (London, 1930), all of which tend to have a boomerang effect by demonstrating how Boswell's arrangement of facts and scenes is often crucial to the Johnsonian portrait.[4]

---

3. Thomas B. Macaulay, "Samuel Johnson," *Fraser's Magazine* (1832).
4. Bertrand Bronson notes this effect in Postgate's collection in "The Double Tradition of Dr. Johnson," in *Johnson Agonistes and Other Essays,* p. 175.

For seventy-five years after the publication in 1856 of Boswell's letters to Temple, the accumulation of new materials, meticulous scholarship, and increasingly sympathetic criticism began to reveal the simplistic nature of Macaulay's judgments. Nevertheless, the shift of critical attention to Boswell's literary artistry was slow until the spectacular discoveries of his private papers at Malahide Castle in Ireland and at Fettercairn House in Scotland. The immediate results of these discoveries were Isham's lavish, privately printed edition of the *Private Papers of James Boswell from Malahide Castle* (1928–34) and a more accurate version of the *Journal of a Tour to the Hebrides* (1936). Drawing on such a wealth of new matter, Geoffrey Scott was able to appreciate Boswell's involved personality perhaps better than even his close friends. More important for the history of literature is Scott's permanently laying to rest the old image of Boswell as a weak-minded, sycophantic reporter surreptitiously taking notes on the spot. All subsequent studies of Boswell draw at least indirectly on Scott's observations to demonstrate the craftsmanship and dramatic quality of the Journals and the *Life*. Frederick Pottle continues not only Scott's editorial labors but also his project of revealing the nature and extent of Boswell's creative powers.

In a sense, of course, Macaulay was right, but Bertrand Bronson, relying on the work of Scott and Pottle, states the paradox in more sympathetic and palatable terms:

It is odd to reflect that if Boswell had been better adjusted, or merely on harmonious terms with his father, there would have been no *Life of Johnson* to delight the world. For in a real sense—though the statement must not stand as a sufficient explanation of that book—the *Life* is the almost involuntary tribute of a great human weakness to a great human strength.[5]

More contemporary readers have felt the need to articulate that "sufficient explanation" of the *Life*. Although all explanations must inevitably fall short, it is a healthy sign in Boswellian scholarship that the *Life* is now being seriously regarded as a product of the creative imagination. Fresh clues to the mystery of the *Life*'s effect may be found in W. K. Wimsatt's all-too-brief study of Boswell's ability to fuse facts and emotions in his Journals, "to take his own emotional temperature, to look forward to his opportunities, and backward to estimate his successes and his failures."[6] This examination and others will be cited in the course of my study.

The basic principles generating the form and style of the *Life* shape the writing of any man who wants to describe and interpret past events, real or fictional. These principles, however, imply a variety of structural and verbal choices, and the individuality of the *Life* emerges as we note Boswell's tendency to make characteristic decisions or to keep certain options open. In dealing with the *Life,* one must remember that Boswell's creativity worked obediently according to the dictates of historical fact and was influenced by many of the practical problems of editing so much material. Then—to use the Romantic version of Plato's allegory—the reader can descend into the cavernous workshop of this exasperating Scot's imagination and later emerge, unblinded, with a clearer vision of his works.

5. Bertrand Bronson, "Boswell's Boswell," in *Johnson Agonistes,* p. 76. Also on this theme is Jeffrey Hart's "Some Thoughts on Johnson as Hero."

6. William K. Wimsatt, Jr., "The Fact Imagined: James Boswell," p. 175.

CHAPTER ONE   *The Temporal*
                      Restlessness of
                      Boswell's Narrative

                              When James Boswell thought
about literary biography in general and his own *Life of
Johnson* in particular, he was, as in almost everything else,
of two minds. Having spent much of his adult life assiduously
copying down his experiences, he was duly impressed with
the impossibility of ever compiling a fully detailed life-record,
even one spanning only a few days. Portrait painters, he says
in his Journal, have it much easier: they can catch in paint
the distinguishing peculiarities of an individual countenance,
whereas a biographer, trying to set down the details of a man's
mind, must deal in words, an imperfect medium. "In the
meantime," he says, "we must be content to enjoy the recollection of characters in our own breasts."[1] In the *Life* itself
Boswell's frequent apologies for the incompleteness of his
record contribute to the never fully submerged elegiac tone
of the work; the *Life* is a vast monument built to the memory
of a man whom Boswell loved very much, but, as he frequently reminds us, a close look at any part of the stonework re-

1. *Boswell: The Ominous Years, 1774–1776*, ed. Charles Ryskamp and
Frederick A. Pottle, p. 168.

veals numerous cracks and fissures indicating the parts of
Johnson that are forever lost in the past.

Boswell's ambivalence about his great project partially
stems from its careless beginnings. After he had met Johnson
in Davies's bookshop in 1763, he gave him a prominent place
in his Journals for the next twenty years. Never abandoning
his ambition to be someday a "great man" (after Johnson's
model, not Walpole's) and yet always aware of how far short
of his goal he was, Boswell probably saw soon that a biography of Johnson was a work that, even more than his projected
dictionary of Scotticisms, would give him an admirable literary reputation. As early as 1765, he wrote to Wilkes from
Venice while on his Grand Tour:

> My veneration and love for that illustrious philosopher is
> so great that I cannot promise to be always free from some
> imitation of him. Could my feeble mind preserve but a
> faint impression of Johnson, it would be a glory to myself
> and a benefit to mankind.[2]

Much later, in 1780, he entered in his Journal: "I told Erskine
I was to write Dr. Johnson's life in scenes. He approved."[3]
However, Boswell apparently did not begin any serious work
on the biography. He became increasingly subject to melan-

2. *Boswell on the Grand Tour: Italy, Corsica, and France, 1765–1766*,
eds. Frank Brady and Frederick A. Pottle, p. 101. Pottle gives a brief
narrative of the planning, collecting for, writing, and printing of the
Life in *The Literary Career of James Boswell, Esq*. Marshall Waingrow
collects all the relevant passages from Boswell's Journal and letters in
"Chronology of the Making of the *Life*," in *The Correspondence and
Other Papers of James Boswell Relating to the Making of the Life of
Johnson*, pp. li–lxxviii.

3. Journal, 12 October 1780; quoted by Geoffrey Scott, "The Making
of the *Life of Johnson*," in *Private Papers of James Boswell from Malahide Castle in the Collection of Lt.-Colonel Ralph Heyward Isham*, eds.
Geoffrey Scott and Frederick A. Pottle, 6: 161.

cholia, and only after Johnson's death in 1784 did he begin, with Malone's encouragement, to write up his Hebridean Journal to test the public's interest in his new method of biography.[4] In 1786 Boswell began working on the *Life* in earnest, again with Malone's prodding, editorial advice, and aid in gathering materials.[5]

Despite his pessimism regarding the completeness of his Journals and perhaps because of the protracted genesis of the *Life,* Boswell opens his great work with the quietly confident remarks of one who has given the problem of biography some thought. He unabashedly justifies his decision to avoid the thousands of editing hours necessary to reduce his Johnsoniana to a uniform point of view: "Instead of melting down my materials into one mass, and constantly speaking in my own person, by which I might have appeared to have more merit in the execution of the work, I have resolved to adopt and enlarge upon the excellent plan of Mr. Mason, in his Memoirs of Gray." He has decided to give a year-by-year account of Johnson's life with reconstructed narrative and "his own minutes, letters, or conversation." In this way, he continues, "my readers [will be] better acquainted with him, than even most of those were who actually knew him, but could know him only partially; whereas there is here an accumulation of intelligence from various points, by which his character is more fully understood and illustrated." "Indeed," he concludes grandly, "I cannot conceive a more perfect mode of writing any man's life, than not only relating all the most important events of it in their order, but interweaving what he privately wrote, and said, and thought; by which mankind are enabled as it were to see him live, and to 'live o'er each

4. Ibid., pp. 161–64.

5. James M. Osborn, "Edmond Malone and Dr. Johnson," in *Johnson, Boswell, and Their Circle: Essays for L. F. Powell,* p. 11.

scene' with him, as he actually advanced through the several stages of his life."[6]

Two ultimately irreconcilable goals are implicit in Boswell's prefatory comments: he wants the *Life* to be both a bulging compendium and a unified narrative. Aware that some were irked by the inclusion of apparent trivia in the *Tour to the Hebrides*, Boswell serves notice that the *Life* has been written on the same principle.

> Of one thing I am certain, that considering how highly the small portion which we have of the table-talk and other anecdotes of our celebrated writers is valued, and how earnestly it is regretted that we have not more, I am justified in preserving rather too many of Johnson's sayings, than too few; especially as from the diversity of dispositions it cannot be known with certainty beforehand, whether what may seem trifling to some, and perhaps to the collector himself, may not be most agreeable to many; and the greater number that an authour can please in any degree, the more pleasure does there arise to a benevolent mind.[7]

Malone's help apparently reinforced Boswell's inclusiveness, for, as Geoffrey Scott points out, "In his unqualified approval of the new biographical method, he is a more convinced Boswellian than Boswell himself."[8] Despite his method and

6. *Life of Samuel Johnson*, ed. G. B. Hill and revised by L. F. Powell, 1: 29–30; subsequently referred to as *Life*, with volume and page numbers following. In the text, entries in the *Life* are referred to by their date, or the nearest datable passage, so that any edition may be used.

7. *Life*, 1: 33–34 (part of undated introduction).

8. Scott, "The Making of the *Life of Johnson*," p. 290. The third edition of the *Life* (1799), which is the basis of the modern Hill-Powell and Tinker-Chapman editions, was put into its final form by Malone, who incorporated after Boswell's death in 1795 the "Additions to Johnson's Life," "Corrections," and "Additional Corrections" appended to the awkwardly arranged second edition of 1793. The question arises, how can we

his respect for the integrity of each contribution to the *Life,* Boswell does make some claims for neatness, perhaps even for a kind of design, in the biography. This attitude is clear in his dismissal of Sir John Hawkins's biography of Johnson as a "farrago," in which "a very small part of it relates to the person who is the subject of the book."[9] Later, in the Advertisement to the second edition, Boswell confides to his readers that in "moments of self-complacency" he thinks of the *Life* as like the *Odyssey* in at least one respect: "Amidst a thousand entertaining and instructive episodes the HERO is never long out of sight; for they are all in some degree connected with him; and HE, in the whole course of the History, is exhibited by the Author for the best advantage of his readers." Earlier, both Fielding and Smollett similarly defined the novel, each having in mind as precedents the episodic structures of the *Odyssey, Orlando Furioso,* and *Don Quixote.*[10]

---

learn about Boswell's style by examining the third edition, which only Malone saw to press? There are two answers. First, Malone's editorial changes were not of the sort that altered the general style of the *Life*. As Malone says in his advertisement in the third edition, he preserved all of Boswell's changes, then distributed the remaining addenda in their proper places, and, with four other men, added many notes. The material to be incorporated numbers only forty-eight pages in the second edition—a small fraction of the third edition's 1877 pages; moreover in *The Principal Corrections and Additions,* 1793, Boswell indicates precisely how the unassigned additions to the second edition are to be inserted in the text (see Pottle, *Literary Career,* pp. 212–14). The second answer is contained in Scott's remark that Malone was more Boswellian than Boswell himself: Malone's changes were in keeping with Boswell's principle of inclusion, a stylistic choice that has prime significance in this study.

Ralph Cohen comments on the additive tendencies in Pope's and Thomson's revisions, in "The Augustan Mode in English Poetry," p. 15.

9. *Life,* 1: 27–28.

10. Fielding distinguishes between the epic with an entire and uniform action (the *Iliad*) and that which is a series of actions tending toward one end (the *Odyssey*), in his "Preface to *David Simple,*" *Works,* ed. W. E.

This twofold nature of the *Life* is the result of Boswell's imaginative apprehension of the past, depending on the twin acts of recall and interpretation.[11] If the *Life* were a work of fiction, most readers would be struck by Boswell's narrative device of habitually recounting a moment of Johnson's life by referring to matters that are chronologically prior or subsequent. In short, Boswell rarely tells his story straight, even when he has sufficient materials to do so. What a reader of the *Life* frequently experiences, even within one sentence, is a whirl of time levels: the historical moment, a time before or after it, the much later time when Boswell was collecting his biographical materials, and the final extended period when he was writing it up and could directly address his audience on various subjects. This lack of chronological stability in the *Life,* and its consequences, are central to this study.

Good examples of Boswell's tendency to mix these time levels can be found in almost any lengthy passage of the *Life,* but in many of the entries covering Johnson's early years Boswell allows the times of his friendship with Johnson and his authorial commentary to intrude upon the historical

---

Henley, 16: 10–11. Smollett's definition of the novel is in his prefatory address to *Ferdinand Count Fathom,* ed. George Saintsbury, 1: 3: "A novel is a large diffused picture, comprehending the characters of life, disposed in different groups, and exhibited in various attitudes, for the purposes of an uniform plan, and general occurrence, to which every individual figure is subservient. But this plan cannot be executed with propriety, probability, or success, without a principal personage to attract the attention, unite the incidents, unwind the clue of the labyrinth, and at last close the scene, by virtue of his own importance."

11. More than once Frederick Pottle has made a case for the role of Boswell's imagination in the Journals and the *Life:* "The Power of Memory in Boswell and Scott," pp. 168–89; "Introduction," *Boswell's London Journal, 1762–1763,* pp. 13–14; and *James Boswell: The Earlier Years, 1740–1769,* pp. 87–92.

moment with exceptional rapidity. In the following selection, describing the two years that Johnson spent at home
after his return from the school at Stourbridge in 1726, the
numbers in brackets provide rough indications of three time
levels: when Boswell is reporting [1], jumping ahead [2], or
commenting authorially [3].

> [1] He had no settled plan of life, nor looked forward
> at all, but merely lived from day to day. Yet he read
> a great deal in a desultory manner, without any scheme
> of study, as chance threw books in his way, and in-
> 5 clination directed him through them. [2] He used to
> mention one curious instance of his casual reading,
> when but a boy. [1] Having imagined that his brother
> had hid some apples behind a large folio upon an upper
> shelf in his father's shop, he climbed up to search for
> 10 them. There were no apples; but the large folio proved
> to be Petrarch, whom he had seen mentioned in some
> preface, as one of the restorers of learning. His curiosity
> having been thus excited, he sat down with avidity,
> and read a great part of the book. [2] What he read
> 15 during these two years he told me, was not works of
> mere amusement, "not voyages and travels, but all
> literature, Sir, all ancient writers, all manly: though
> but little Greek, only some of Anacreon and Hesiod;
> but in this irregular manner (added he) I had looked
> 20 into a great many books, which were not commonly
> known at the Universities, where they seldom read
> any books but what are put into their hands by their
> tutors. . . ."
> [3] In estimating the progress of his mind during
> 25 these two years, as well as in future periods of his life,
> we must not regard his own hasty confession of idle-
> ness; for we see, [2] when he explains himself, that

he was acquiring various stores; and, indeed, he himself concluded the account with saying, "I would not
30 have you think I was doing nothing then." [1725–28]

The bracketed numbers do not do full justice to the subtle
mixture of time levels. Jumping ahead in lines 5–7 ("He used
to mention . . . "), Boswell tags the end of the sentence with
"when but a boy" to insure that the reader is still focused
on Johnson as a boy during 1726–28. Furthermore, "He used
to mention" suggests a repeated story-telling, not merely an
event occurring in only one point of time. Quickly, Boswell's
narrative sets the scene and establishes better than before
the immediacy of the past moment (lines 7–14). Even more
quickly however, he dissolves this immediacy by quoting
Johnson when he was looking back to this event (lines 16–23),
and, just as we have begun to recapture through his own
words a picture of the young Johnson, now devouring almost
every classical author in sight, Boswell again yanks us ahead
to this story-telling time with a parenthetical "added he"
(line 19). In the next paragraph Boswell's chief aim is to pull
the reader away from not only the historical moment but
also the time of Johnson's speaking, this new distance being
the result of Boswell's wanting to share with his readers his
response to this anecdote. For this reason, lines 24–30 are a
tangle of temporal references ranging from the original events
through Johnson's immediate and later future up to Boswell's
moment of writing the *Life*.

Boswell violates the onward flow of his narrative in ways
that do not fall into a general pattern. He may withdraw
from the historical moment to observe its larger significance,
or he may allow outside details to intrude temporarily upon
an intimate scene that he has been building. A good example
of the latter is the account of Boswell's meeting Johnson
alone in his study after a Good Friday evening service. The

time is a quiet one, but Boswell interrupts his record of Johnson's ruminations on immortality to follow up a *bon mot* uttered later by Topham Beauclerk, and then returns to the scene and subject (14 April 1775). Such disquieting interruptions do occur in the *Life,* making many modern readers wish that some of this material had been relegated to the footnotes. To be sure, no critical analysis of the *Life* can justify all of these abrupt switches in time; to do so would be special pleading which ignores the fact that Boswell occasionally undermines his own best effects, as when he departs from his account of his first visit to Johnson's rooms to record a few words about Smart that Johnson and Dr. Burney exchanged at some unspecified prior or subsequent time.

The dramatic immediacy of the *Life* constantly changes, both because of these interruptions and because of the frequent shift of narrator and documents. As the point of view becomes increasingly remote from the historical moment, the result may have one of two opposite effects: the subject (Johnson) is someone observed from afar, of whose story we can perceive only a fragment, or he is seen in great clarity by a narrator who is aware of many events (and therefore several time levels) in the subject's history. This second point of view is a qualified omniscience, because Boswell and some of Johnson's other friends had perspectives of the man that are real-life approximations of the impossible knowledge that an omniscient author has in fiction. Of course, if Boswell or one of his guest narrators chooses to report an event in detail, then a spatial intimacy accompanies the temporal immediacy of his record. The reader tacitly (and fallaciously) reasons to himself, "One can spin out general descriptions and evaluations of Johnson from hearsay while alone in one's study, but to record an event in any detail requires that one must have been in the same room with him."

Throughout the *Life* the reader's sense of Boswell's authority, as well as the dramatic immediacy, changes cyclically:
his intimate knowledge of many men's pasts makes the reader
feel that he is in the sure hands of an almost omniscient narrator—an illusion which is dispelled as soon as Boswell complains of the inadequacy of his records, but which begins
growing again until the next complaint. The absolutism of
the term "omniscience" can be avoided by using the more
workable term "privilege."[12] There are degrees of privileged
narrators, ranging from the (usually) omniscient "Fielding,"
the implied author of *Tom Jones,* to the severely limited
"Henry James" who sees the action of *The Ambassadors*
through the eyes of Lambert Strether. And modern novelists,
such as Joyce and Robbe-Grillet, have pushed these extremes
back even further.[13]

Pauses in the onward progression of a narrative, together
with their consequences for point of view, are not unusual in
eighteenth-century fiction and biography. Although Tristram
Shandy is admittedly an extremist in these matters, his skit-
tishness in telling his life story is a response to the same conflict between chronology and meaning that Boswell, or any
historian, faces. Solving this problem at a woeful cost to
dramatic immediacy, Sir John Hawkins, one of Boswell's
rival biographers, consistently treats Johnson as a distant
object of historical study; since he maintains a quite even
distance from the events he describes, his commentary and
his narrative do not sharply contrast in their proximity to
the historical moment.[14] The reader of Hawkins's biography

12. Wayne Booth, "Distance and Point-of-View: An Essay in Classification," pp. 60–79.
13. Bruce Morrissette, "The Evolution of Narrative Viewpoint in
Robbe-Grillet," pp. 24–33.
14. When Boswell's *Life* was published in 1791, it was following seven
other biographies of Johnson: Thomas Tyers's *Biographical Sketch of
Dr. Samuel Johnson* (1785), previously published in *The Gentleman's*

of Johnson is not subjected to the Boswellian mixture of time levels simply because no variety of levels is clearly realized. Hawkins's inability or unwillingness to create detailed scenes, together with his plodding legalistic prose and his incorrigibly long digressions, makes his work a rambling essay occasioned by Johnson's life story rather than a biography whose very substance is that story. This difference is ultimately one of tone, the writer's attitude toward his subject. Nowhere does Boswell sound as mechanical and cold as Hawkins does here, slicing up Johnson's life and character as if they were a loaf of bread:

> The life I am now writing seems to divide itself into two periods; the first marked by a series of afflictions, the last by some cheering rays of comfort and comparative affluence. Johnson, at this time [1745–50], had passed nearly half of his days: here, therefore, let me make a stand, and having hitherto represented him in his literary, endeavour to exhibit him in his religious, moral, and economical character, adverting first to such particulars respecting the course of life he had chosen, and the evils to which it exposed him, as seem properly to belong to the first member of the above division.[15]

Hawkins's lack of concern for Johnson's diurnal activity may be seen in his decision to divide the biography into sections covering from two to seven years; often it is impossible to

---

Magazine; The Life of Samuel Johnson, LL.D. (1785), attributed to William Cook; Rev. William Shaw's *Memoirs of the Life and Writings of The Late Dr. Samuel Johnson* (1785); Mrs. Piozzi's *Anecdotes of the Late Samuel Johnson, LL.D.* (1786); Joseph Towers's *Essay on the Life, Character, and Writings of Dr. Samuel Johnson* (1786); and Sir John Hawkins's *Life of Johnson* (1787).

15. Sir John Hawkins, Knt., *The Life of Samuel Johnson, LL.D.*, ed. and abridged by Bertram H. Davis, p. 68.

unravel the relative chronology of events within a given section.

It would have been disappointing if Boswell, guilty of inconsistency on so many counts, had adopted Hawkins's even and detached viewpoint. He was unwilling to reconstruct a third-person account in which he either suppressed all references to events outside the historical moment or, like Hawkins, wrote about each of Johnson's experiences solely as *exempla* of moral universals. In the *Life of Johnson* Boswell alternates between both of these methods, a decision forced on him by the wide variety of his biographical materials and by the various personal attitudes toward his subject that he includes in his record.

Thus, two narrative elements—Boswell's materials and authorial interventions—are responsible in the *Life* for intrusions of time levels other than that of the historical moment. Each element has many parts, which, taken together, form a temporal continuum ranging from the historical moment to the time of composition. A closer look at these materials and interventions provides clues to the wayward thematic and stylistic unity that Boswell achieved in the *Life*.

The biographical materials confronting Boswell as he wrote the *Life* fall into five categories.[16] First, he had some very rough memoranda that had never been written up in the Journals. Second, there were many condensed notes and "papers apart," both of which needed organization. Next, Boswell had to cope with his voluminous Journals, which spanned most of his adulthood and in which Johnson's story was conflated with irrelevant Boswelliana; the separation of one from the other must have loomed as a task of intimidating proportions. Furthermore, Boswell had a few note-

16. These five types are mentioned by Geoffrey Scott in "The Making of the *Life of Johnson*," p. 184.

books, like the one in which he kept the pre-1763 Johnsoniana that he had gleaned at various times. Finally, he had a large stock, which he increased after Johnson's death, of letters, copied documents, and contributions submitted by members of the Doctor's circle and other acquaintances. Examples of these materials are Johnson's notebook of his travels in France (10 Oct.–5 Nov. 1775); Francis Barber's account of Johnson's sorrow after his wife's death (1752); Thomas Warton's description of Johnson's visit to Oxford (summer 1754); Bennet Langton's Johnsoniana, edited and partially rewritten by Boswell for stylistic reasons (included under 1780); and a series of imitations of Johnson's style by diverse hands (Nov.–Dec. 1784). In addition to these unassimilated contributions, the *Life* includes hundreds of details with documented sources; indeed, Boswell considerably strained his friendship with Thomas Percy when he flatly refused to allow the bishop to remain an anonymous contributor to the *Life*.[17]

These materials are accounts or evaluations drawn from the experience of dozens of people whom readers become aware of as mediating sensibilities between them and the past. This awareness increases when Boswell in his transitions briefly describes these contributors and even the ways in which they came to offer their information; in other words, there is rudimentary characterization and dramatization. The account of Johnson's discovery of Petrarch in his father's shop shows Boswell's tendency to divide the reader's attention: an image of young Sam Johnson alternates with that of the older man telling the tale to Boswell many years later.

Some of the materials mentioned above, such as the French notebook and Barber's story, are, along with the letters, relatively immediate records of past moments or mental states

17. The ramifications of this relationship are explored by C. N. Fifer in "Boswell and the Decorous Bishop," pp. 48–56.

experienced by Johnson. Other contributions, such as Burney's and most of Langton's, include Johnsonian pronouncements that tend to be isolated from any historical, social, or psychological detail. Such passages are like Hawkins's generalities except that they are closer to Johnson's spoken idiom. The full range of these materials establishes at least four time levels: the original moment(s), a middle time (or perhaps one prior to the historical moment), the period when Boswell was gathering papers for the *Life,* and the final time when he was writing, standing apart from history and addressing his audience on the timeless significance of the Johnsonian drama.

Boswell's principle of inclusion swelled the quantity of his biographical materials, and his reverence for authenticity as well as his desire to finish the *Life* rapidly disposed him to assemble rather than "melt down" these papers. Further inclining him to respect the integrity of each contribution was his childlike delight in different views of Johnson, a variety that was evidence of the man's complexity, a multifaceted reality that lay beyond words. That Boswell loved the aura of mystery surrounding Johnson is clear in the limp and rather unconvincing scolding that he gives himself in his Journal one evening after the two of them had met for the first time in over five months:

> We were quite easy, quite as Companions tonight. But so ready is my mind to suggest matter for dissatisfaction, that I had a sort of regret that we were so easy. I missed that aweful reverence with which I used to contemplate *Mr. Samuel Johnson* in the complex Magnitude of his Literary, Moral, & Religious character. I have a wonderful superstitious love of *Mystery,* when perhaps the truth is that it is owing to the darkness of my own mind. I should be glad that

I am more advanced in my progress of being, so that I can view Dr. Johnson with a steadier and clearer eye. My dissatisfaction tonight was foolish. Would it not be foolish to regret that we shall have less mystery in a future state? That we now "see as in a glass, darkly," but shall "then see face to face"?[18]

It is this primitive wonder at Johnson's complexity, together with his desire to use other men to supplement his cloudy vision, that led Boswell to leave intact most of his materials: Johnson's prayers and meditations, recorded conversations, the letters, first-person accounts (including Boswell's), reconstructed narrative, and general comments on Johnson and biography. The latter are authorial interventions serving as a reminder that the distinction between "materials" and "authorial roles" does break down even though it is temporarily helpful; in fact, this breaking down is the chief source of the reader's impression that the *Life* is an authoritative, artless record.

An examination of the use of Johnson's *Prayers and Meditations* in the *Life* demonstrates how Boswell offers a series of now near, now far glimpses of Johnson and uses these to orchestrate the reader's various reactions, positive and negative, into an overall sympathetic response much like that he would have to a good friend whose shortcomings he knows well. Johnson is presented in a constant series of shifts between his public and private life, between his past and present, between his internal turbulence and outward calm, and between the reader as spectator and the subject as suffer-

18. Journal in Edinburgh and London, 20 March 1778, pp. 45–46; this section is transcribed in Inge Probstein's "Boswell's London Journal of 1778," pp. 12–13; and in *Boswell in Extremes, 1776–1778,* ed. Charles McC. Weis and F. A. Pottle, p. 225. See also the slightly altered version in the *Life.*

er.[19] Even though Johnson's *Prayers and Meditations,* published shortly after his death by the Reverend George Strahan, are an utterly trustworthy record, their topical and emotional range is severely limited, thus inviting Boswell to add to their intense subjectivity a descant-like commentary or a contrapuntal topic.

To illustrate Johnson's ceaseless desire for intellectual improvement despite his increasingly painful bodily and mental complications, Boswell offers a list of the old man's wide reading and then, a few pages later, quotes the *Prayers and Meditations* to reveal the undue severity with which Johnson judged himself: " 'This year has passed with so little improvement, that I doubt whether I have not rather impaired than increased my learning'; and yet we have seen how he *read,* and we know how he *talked* during that period" (1 Jan. 1744).[20]

A variation on this technique occurs when Boswell uses the *Prayers and Meditations* (or any other close-up view of Johnson) to establish the Doctor's personal troubles and then follows with some of his letters in which he reveals a more

19. The following is a list of the places in the *Life* where Boswell quotes or overtly refers to the *Prayers and Meditations,* with an asterisk next to the references that do not use the source in the ways that I have mentioned. In these latter cases, which are a minority of the total number, Boswell most often uses the book simply as a source of biographical detail.

    Late 1730*, 9 July 1735*, July 1755*, 1 Jan. 1756*, April 1758, March 1759*, early 1760*, beginning 1761, 20–21 April 1764, beginning 1765, 26 Sept. 1765, Sept. 1765, 18 Oct. 1767, beginning 1769, 1 June 1770, Oct. 1771, 18 April 1772, 1 Jan. 1774, 14 April 1775, 25 July 1776, beginning 1777, 17 April 1778*, 4 April 1781, autumn 1781, 20 Jan. 1782*, 2 March 1782, 6 Oct. 1782, mid-Nov. 1784, early Dec. 1784.

20. Boswell uses this public-private contrast later when he is recounting Johnson's last days and protecting his lifelong integrity against the scattered charges of hypocrisy. To demonstrate Johnson's radical sincerity and humility, he uses the longest series in the *Life* of quotations from the *Prayers and Meditations* (early Dec. 1784).

public self to his acquaintances. Two passages demonstrate this pattern. Boswell begins his account for 1770 with Johnson's publication of *The False Alarm,* a political pamphlet justifying the ministry's removal of Wilkes from Parliament and attempting to play down the move as any threat to the public's right of election. Though he does see a few good things in the work, he admits to its basic wrongheadedness. Immediately following is a remarkably abrupt transition in which, after summarizing the bitter replies to *The False Alarm,* Boswell says that Johnson

> was, however, soothed in the highest strain of panegyrick, in a poem called "The Remonstrance," by the Rev. Mr. Stockdale, to whom he was, upon many occasions, a kind protector.
>
> The following admirable minute made by him describes so well his own state, and that of numbers to whom self-examination is habitual, that I cannot omit it:—
>
> "June 1, 1770. Every man naturally persuades himself that he can keep his resolutions, nor is he convinced of his imbecility but by length of time and frequency of experiment...."

The quoted section continues as an atypically objective description of Johnson's failures of will.

A number of things are significant here. First, the objectively described and temporally diffuse ("upon many occasions") pamphlet episode starkly contrasts with the private reflections pinpointed in time by "June 1, 1770." That this self-portrait is unusually impersonal for Johnson's private papers is a sign of his extreme personal anguish, for this is one of Johnson's quiet, heroic attempts to make sense out of the chaos of his constant backsliding by drawing a soothing generalization that will link his behavior to that of other men. The abrupt change in subject matter, together with the contrasts in time and immediacy, has brought about a change in our sympathies. By this time, quite early in the *Life,* Boswell is already emphasizing Johnson's full commitment to the law of subordination and suggesting the connection between his Toryism and his concern for personal resolution and will power; the result is that a reader can now understand if not subscribe to his reasons for writing *The False Alarm.*

Another harsh transition follows this long excerpt from the *Prayers and Meditations:* Boswell states blandly, "Of this year I have obtained the following letters" and then includes three letters from Johnson concerning the revision with Steevens of his Shakespeare edition and two kind notes from him to Francis Barber. These materials—the pamphlet episode, the personal reflections, and the letters—constitute everything available to Boswell for 1770; the rest of the year is filled out with Maxwell's *Collectanea,* anecdotal snippets gathered over a number of years. Boswell admits that he is using this compilation to compensate for the "total cessation of all correspondence between Dr. Johnson and me."

Because the materials are so sparse, Boswell's arrangement of them is especially important: first the pamphlet affair, something about which he had only secondhand information, then the intimate view of Johnson, and finally a retreat to the middle distance with Johnson's letters of paternal affection for his servant and his cordial requests to fellow scholars concerning his work in progress. Thus the stage is set and the man's emotional weather described before the man is presented in his more public self. Also, *The False Alarm* affair has been placed in a larger perspective, something that would have been more difficult if it had come last in the entry for 1770.

The end of the section for 1771 is a similar example of this method. Johnson's pathetic self-lacerations are first described generally, as if spread over much time; then, as the *Prayers and Meditations* are quoted, his sorrows become more fixed in time, only to become increasingly diffuse again as the authorial commentary intrudes. To use a spatial metaphor, a moderate expansiveness is followed by a contraction and finally by an expansion of even greater proportions. The full passage is necessary to demonstrate this movement, which is not at all uncommon in the *Life*.

In his religious record of this year, we observe that he was better than usual, both in body and mind, and better satisfied with the regularity of his conduct. But he is still "trying his ways" too rigorously. He charges himself with not rising early enough; yet he mentions what was surely a sufficient excuse for this, supposing it to be a duty seriously required, as he all his life appears to have thought it. "One great hindrance is want of rest; my nocturnal complaints grow less troublesome towards morning; and I am tempted to repair the deficiencies of the night." Alas! how hard it would be if this indulgence were to be imputed to a sick man as a crime. In his retrospect on the following Easter-Eve, he says, "When I review the last year, I am able to recollect so little done, that shame and sorrow, though perhaps too weakly, come upon me." Had he been judging of any one else in the same circumstances, how clear would he have been on the favorable side. How very difficult, and in my opinion, almost constitutionally impossible it was for him to be raised early, even by the strongest resolutions, appears from a note in one of his little paper-books, (containing words arranged for his *Dictionary*,) written, I suppose, about 1753: "I do not remember that since I left Oxford I ever rose early by mere choice, but once or twice at Edial, and two or three times for the *Rambler*." I think he had fair ground enough to have quieted his mind on this

subject, by concluding that he was physically incapable of
what is at best but a commodious regulation. [End of
1771]

One may object that Boswell is not doing anything especially intricate here: he is introducing a point, supporting
it with concrete examples, and closing with the same point in
a more elaborate form and seen in larger perspective. And in
fact, with his many years of legal practice behind him, he is
more prone to this pattern than most people—so prone, indeed, that this trait actually becomes idiosyncratic. In the
Life, the alternation of authorial and historical time levels
gives Johnson's situation a full and sympathetic treatment
and makes his letters part of his daily life rather than obliquely relevant documents. And again, as in the story of *The False
Alarm,* the effect of this juxtaposition of materials is heightened by an abrupt transition: "In 1772 he was altogether
quiescent as an authour; but it will be found from the various
evidences which I shall bring together that his mind was
acute, lively, and vigorous." Although Boswell establishes
similar contrasts with other materials, his use of Johnson's
private papers is especially clear-cut, since they are at the extreme end of the time-continuum on which all of the biographical materials can be located. The mixing of time levels
in the *Life* is a complex phenomenon, however; it is the result
of not only these varied materials but also Boswell's ways of
intruding himself into his narrative.

Boswell's blatant authorial interventions are only the most
noticeable way, next to his actual appearances in scenes, in
which he becomes visible to the reader. A closer look at the
Life reveals Boswell in a large number of stances that either
are implicit in his materials or arise in direct response to

them.[21] Following his general principle of contrast, of seldom anchoring his narrative in one time level, he sometimes finds that relatively intimate historical documents provoke an intrusion. Or, the reverse may happen, and an Olympian observation on Johnson may provide the occasion for including records in which the original event is vividly realized.

Boswell offers his readers many representations of himself partially because his sense of his own identity is fragmented; in Bertrand Bronson's words, "the multiplicity of his potentialities bewilders him."[22] In his Journals he sought to stabilize his personality, to see a pattern in the flux of his everyday behavior, and to form an ideal image of himself toward which he could strive. His long, desperate search for a fixed personality and his dread of an annihilated identity are clear in two striking, widely spaced Journal entries in which he sees his individuality melted down like wax or metal in a fire.[23] He uses the same language to describe his editing of

21. "Role" or "pose" are misleading terms because they imply artificiality or even a falsification of one's own responses and personality. Similarly, the fashionable "persona" is dangerous because it connotes a consciously constructed and sustained literary role. Each side of Boswell that we see in the *Life* was part of his historical personality, but his authorial attitudes are too fragmented to coalesce into a psychologically coherent "implied author." His responses tend to become compartmentalized so that we have Boswell the rake, the lawyer, the moralist, and so forth. Insofar as he was aware of these divisions and even cultivated their various superficial mannerisms, each side is self-conscious, but insofar as each division was a genuine potential in the personality whose unity he strained to discern, each side was unartificial. Although there is no perfect term for these divisions, "stance" is the best that I can think of.

22. Bertrand Bronson, "Boswell's Boswell," p. 403.

23. *Boswell in Holland, 1763–1764*, ed. Frederick A. Pottle, p. 281; and *Boswell for the Defence, 1769–1774*, eds. W. K. Wimsatt, Jr. and Frederick A. Pottle, p. 100. Boswell is extremely defensive in the second entry: "I should not wish to be melted so as not to be again separated from the mass."

the *Life:* "Instead of melting down my materials into one mass . . ." Perhaps Boswell associated the loss of individuality (his own or Johnson's) with the reduction of his Johnsoniana to a uniform point of view. Despite his affirmations to the contrary, he feared the loss of his selfhood for most of his adult life. David Hume, whose works Boswell read with fascinated horror, probably heightened the seriousness of this threat by asserting that the notion of personal identity is a comforting chimera that man has invented to blind him to the chaos of his internal life.[24]

Before the section for 1763 Boswell has already represented himself to his readers many times, but with great self-consciousness he announces his entrance into Johnson's life: "This is to me a memorable year." Now he can show himself as part of the historical moment, conversing, dining, and striving to make his mark in the world. Soon he tells his readers of his frustrated attempt to meet Johnson through Thomas Sheridan, and, after the meeting in Davies's bookshop, he describes his efforts to see Johnson again, his failure to secure a commission in the Foot Guards, and his decision to please his father by studying law at Utrecht. His justification for including some of these details is personal: "My readers will, I trust, excuse me for being thus minutely circumstantial, when it is considered that the acquaintance of Dr. Johnson was to me a most valuable acquisition" (13 June 1763). And finally, as Johnson's asthma and dropsy are taking their toll, leaving him little more than a month to live,

24. In his *Treatise of Human Nature* (1740) Hume claims that when we look into ourselves we discover only a fleeting train of distinct perceptions which have no inherent connection (1: vi–vii). Boswell never succeeds in dispelling this Humean nightmare. His criticisms of this "skeptical cobweb" are the defensive outbursts of one who would like to wish away the dilemma and substitute instead grand, positive assertions; see *Boswell on the Grand Tour: Germany and Switzerland, 1764*, ed. Frederick A. Pottle, pp. 28, 179.

Boswell announces his retreat to the wings: "I now relieve the readers of this Work from any farther personal notice of its authour, who if he should be thought to have obtruded himself too much upon their attention, requests them to consider the peculiar plan of his biographical undertaking" (3 Nov. 1784). This remark is the literary counterpart of Boswell's final good-bye to Johnson about five months earlier; the first leave-taking occurs one June night in Reynolds's coach, the second is spoken in Boswell's heart, as if to say, "Johnson is now alone in his private suffering, and our earthly bond has been broken."

Each of Boswell's self-representations, whether obvious or implicit, reveals him in a particular stance, and these stances, like the parade of materials in the *Life,* form a time continuum stretching from the historical moment up to the time of composition. The interplay of these time levels follows the principle of contrast already noted in the arrangement of materials. Boswell's tendency to move into, and then away from, the historical moment can be seen even in his Journals, where he vacillates between participating in events and stepping back to judge his behavior according to his conscience, the corrective faculty that internalized most of what he took to be his society's moral values.[25] Just as an examination of Boswell's use of his materials reveals this movement in the overall portrait of Johnson, so a brief survey of the authorial stances, working progressively away from the historical moment, indicates a temporal restlessness in our views of Boswell. These multiple views frequently give the reader the eerie pleasure of sensing Boswell at his side, enjoying himself from the gallery, even when he is in the thick of the action.

The *Life* omits a tremendous amount of Journal matter.

25. W. K. Wimsatt, Jr., in "The Fact Imagined: James Boswell," pp. 181–82, argues for Boswell's moral self-awareness, or at least his constant return to such a state after acting obtusely.

Other than the scenes with Johnson, Boswell gives us only glimpses of his own hectic life in 1763: angling for a commission in the guards, looking for his main chance in London society, and carrying on various amours in parallel as well as in series. It is primarily as the friend of Johnson that we see him most deeply involved in the historical moment. Most of the scenes between the two men which include their conversation were lifted intact or expanded by Boswell from his Journals, or else greatly expanded from condensed notes and rough memoranda. In these scenes Boswell is revealed as Johnson's sympathetic listener, dogged debater, willing straight man, and skillful interviewer. The following memorable exchange occurred 26 October 1769.

> I know not how so whimsical a thought came into my mind, but I asked, "If, Sir, you were shut up in a castle, and a newborn child with you, what would you do?" JOHNSON. "Why, Sir, I should not much like my company." BOSWELL. "But would you take the trouble of rearing it?" He seemed, as may well be supposed, unwilling to pursue the subject: but upon my persevering in my question, replied, "Why yes, Sir, I would.... I would not *coddle* the child. No, Sir, the hardy method of treating children does no good...." BOSWELL. "Would you teach this child that I have furnished you with, anything?" JOHNSON. "No, I should not be apt to teach it." BOSWELL. "Would not you have a pleasure in teaching it?" JOHNSON. "No, Sir, I should *not* have a pleasure in teaching it." BOSWELL. "Have you not a pleasure in teaching men?—*There* I have you. You have the same pleasure in teaching men, that I should have in teaching children." JOHNSON. "Why, something about that." [26 Oct. 1769]

In the entries before 1763 Boswell frequently violates the chronology of his narrative to refer or appeal to his friendship with Johnson. These intrusions may be short, such as "I heard Johnson say this," or they may be longer and more personal, as when he comments on "The Vanity of Human Wishes": "I am not satisfied if a year passes without my having read it through; and at every perusal, my admiration of the mind which produced it is so highly raised, that I can scarcely believe that I had the honour of enjoying the intimacy of such a man" (April 1759). A few sentences later Boswell observes that Johnson's melancholic constitution made him see life with unusual grimness, "for I am sure that he had less enjoyment from it than I have" (April 1759). The cumulative effect of these pre-1763 intrusions is to establish for the reader the closeness of their relationship as quickly as possible, so that he can enjoy the transactions of friendship as soon as they meet. This device also serves to increase Boswell's authority as a biographer and to give his friendship with Johnson the sprawling, time-transcending quality that he clearly felt it had. Boswell's stance as the friend of Johnson, therefore, involves varying degrees of dramatic immediacy and several time levels, each of which emerges from a different side of their friendship.

A few times Boswell interrupts his story to inform his audience of similar events that he himself participated in, often without Johnson, events that occurred in the middle distance between the historical moment and the composition of the *Life*. In detailing Johnson's early career with *The Gentleman's Magazine,* he mentions his own fondness for *The Scots Magazine* (March 1738); after presenting one of Johnson's prayers for the divine care of his dead wife, he refers to the passing of his own wife in 1789 (17 March 1752); and as a defense of Johnson's criticisms of Scotland in the *Journey to the Western Islands of Scotland* he assures his readers that he, as a patriotic Scot and a citizen of the world, would be the first to sense an injustice if any existed (early 1775). The stances that emerge from these remarks, however, occur often in the *Life* and innumerable times in the Journals and letters: Boswell the young author (or later, the man of letters), the mourning husband, the loyal Scot, and the citizen of the world.[26] These Boswells arise from events, sudden and diffuse, that comprise the fragmented Boswellian experience, which stretches out before, during, and after the historical moment.

There is also in the *Life* a group of authorial stances which are near the end of the continuum, approaching the time of composition: they represent (in order of decreasing dramatic immediacy) Boswell the defender of Johnson, the individual, the moralist, and the biographer. Boswell appears before his readers in these stances with greater frequency than he appears in the recorded conversations. During the resulting pauses in the narrative action, the reader becomes aware that Boswell is writing after the whole real-life story has ended; all that is left is getting the facts together and judging them properly.

It was natural for Boswell to take a stand as Johnson's defender. He had a deep affection for the old scholar and, for professional and personal reasons, he wanted to discredit the Johnsonian biographies by Mrs. Piozzi and Hawkins, both published in 1786. As a rival, he sought to disqualify them as authoritative sources of Johnsoniana and as fair judges of Johnson the man. He counters many erroneous charges, such

26. Boswell's efforts to live like a Spanish grandee are noted by Pottle in *James Boswell: The Earlier Years, 1740–1769*, pp. 148, 303, 318. The most egregious example of Boswell's ignoring his narrative to concentrate on his own career is his handling of Johnson's letter complimenting the Boswellian Journal more highly than the *Account of Corsica*. Never one to accept praise gracefully, Boswell appends to this letter a long footnote from the *Account* rhapsodizing over the tremendous personal satisfaction one has in being an author (autumn 1769). The quotation is an interesting example of young Boswell's unfettered idealism, but it is hardly an integral part of Johnson's life story.

as the view that Johnson was a foolish believer in ghosts (25 June 1763). Elsewhere in the *Life* he clears Johnson on several counts: of mean and jealous peevishness when Thomas Sheridan got his pension (beginning 1763); of moral laxity (5 April 1772, early Dec. 1784); of undiscriminating abhorrence of Milton (30 April 1773 and note); of idleness—his own charge (May–July 1773); of harsh bearishness (end of 1751, 25 June 1763, beginning 1774, 23 March 1776, 1 June 1784); of not loving his wife (March 1752); and of pharisaical over-scrupulousness in religion (early Dec. 1784).

In refuting these claims and many others, Boswell is eager to demonstrate that his defenses are not merely the feelings of a weak-minded, wide-eyed partisan. To this end, his judgments of Johnson often involve fine discriminations in which he admits definite shortcomings in the Doctor's character. Such passages establish Boswell as a reliable narrator, but they also satisfy his urge to assert himself as a fully independent sensibility with opinions and reactions that are his own, not borrowed. Thus, Boswell occasionally steps outside the narrative of the *Life* to criticize or disagree with Johnson, usually on literature, politics, or his behavior. Boswell tempers or disagrees with Johnson on Lord Chesterfield's letters (early 1754 and note), Gray's poetry (25 June 1763), Churchill's poetry (1 July 1763), Derrick's writings (28 July 1763), and Fielding's novels (spring 1768, 6 April 1772). Also, Boswell has dissenting opinions on Robert Walpole (May 1738), Lord Lovat (April 1747 and note), Rousseau (15 Feb. 1766), and Lord Marchmont (early 1781). Occasionally Boswell even criticizes the man himself. In some of Johnson's political pamphlets, such as *The Patriot,* he saw "amidst many powerful arguments, not only a considerable portion of sophistry, but a contemptuous ridicule of his opponents, which was very provoking" (Oct. 1774). Although most of these intrusions reveal Boswell's fairness and powers of judgment, all

too often he asserts his individuality in embarrassing self-justi-
fications that arise from his defensiveness and pride.[27] These
unhappy passages suggest the dark side of the manic zeal that
led to the vast collection of Johnsoniana in the first place.

When Boswell becomes the moralizer, the Greek chorus to
his narrative, he draws even further away from the events of
Johnson's life. After his critique of *Rasselas,* Boswell delivers
a short sermon-digression on the possibility of enjoyment in
this vale of tears, ending with a rather bathetic Johnsonian
imitation: "But if we walk with hope in 'the mid-day sun' of
revelation, our temper and disposition will be such, that the
comforts and enjoyments in our way will be relished, while
we patiently support the inconveniences and pains" (April
1759). In this recurring moralistic tone, which echoes the
manner of the eighteenth-century essayists, Boswell seems to
be striving for the ease of Addison and the authority of Johnson. This reconciliation is impossible, and Boswell's successes
in that vein occur in the moments when one of them is his exclusive model. However, his moralizing generally lacks the
sureness of touch found in the recorded conversations and in
the stances that show him as primarily a participant rather
than a judge. In the manuscript of the *Life* the majority of
revisions are to be found in these evaluative passages.

As biographer, Boswell often emphasizes the necessity of
using historical records and the difficulty that may attend
acquiring them. He takes this stance every time he says something like "I have in my possession, by the favour of Mr. John

27. Four examples are sufficient to give one the flavor of these intrusions: "Had I not been honoured with a very kind and partial notice in
it . . . " (late 1756); "I fully intended to have followed advice of such
weight . . . " (note to 28 July 1763); "He did not favour me with a single
letter for more than two years, for which it will appear that he after-
wards apologized" (end of 1765); and "I am, with all deference, going to
offer a few observations in defense of my Latin, which you have found
fault with. . . . I have defended myself as well as I could" (6 Nov. 1766).

Nichols, a paper in Johnson's hand-writing . . ." (summer 1738), or "The particulars of this conversation I have been at great pains to collect . . ." (note to early Feb. 1767). Every time Boswell says that "we see that Johnson was doing such-and-such a thing at a given time," he shows himself almost as greatly removed from the historical moment as are his readers. Whenever he apologizes for the incompleteness of his narrative, especially of his recorded conversations, he stands before his readers as a frustrated biographer. The literary detective and the writer-craftsman are the two basic forms of the biographer's stance, and whether Boswell's use of this stance is fleeting or sustained, the effect is roughly the same: the narrative temporarily makes room for an image of the older Boswell searching for certain papers or information and referring self-consciously to his pride and tribulations in being a biographer, a man of letters.

To generalize from this evidence, the stances closest to the historical action are usually those that are implicit in the biographical materials, whereas those further removed are reactions to the materials. The alternations of time levels and points of view that gradually generate a composite portrait of Johnson also work through Boswell's stances to evoke a comparable portrait of the artist. The relationship between the materials and the stances has been indicated but not analyzed—an impossible task because of the randomness with which Boswell sometimes uses materials that involve particular stances and stances that call to mind certain materials. All that can be said is that these two narrative elements exist in a reciprocal, symbiotic relationship in which each has the power to evoke the other. In this series of oscillations there is no grand pattern in the massing of materials or stances, and neither Johnson nor Boswell develops into something that is not already seen in the first few hundred pages of the work. Some sections, such as the Johnson-Boswell conversations, are both materials and stances because of the rapidity with which Boswell switches back and forth between his desire to represent Johnson and his desire to represent himself, each man in all his complexity. Thus, despite their being intricately mingled, the temporary separation of these two narrative elements makes clearer how they articulate the two main subjects of the *Life,* Samuel Johnson and Boswell's friendship with him.

CHAPTER TWO

Johnson and Form:
A Monument
For Posterity

Boswell's aim in writing the
Life has not always been clear. An obvious implication of
Macaulay's view (though not expressed by him) is that this
rather pathetic braying jackass of a Scotsman wrote the
Life primarily to display himself before the public. Poor
Johnson had been reduced to a means of satisfying Boswell's need for the limelight.[1] The discovery of Boswell's
Journals has deprived this viewpoint of any respectability
since they reveal how often and with what almost always
good judgment Boswell suppressed references to himself in
the *Life*.[2] Boswell's reason for writing the *Life,* the most

1. In only slightly more temperate language, this is the main thesis
of Percy Fitzgerald's *Boswell's Autobiography.*

2. "It has sometimes been suggested that one of Boswell's motives in
writing the *Life* was to find opportunities of airing his own conversation
and reflections. The Journals decidedly contradict this aspersion. The
excisions constantly prove the sincerity of Boswell's claim that only what
led up to and drew forth Johnson's talk, or illuminated his character,
could be admitted to the work. Considering the essentially egoistic nature
of the Journals from which Boswell was working, it is remarkable how
few exceptions to this rule have been suffered to creep in" (Geoffrey
Scott, "The Making of the *Life of Johnson,*" p. 190).

laborious project he ever undertook, was to get down on paper as completely as possible a vast record of Johnson's life, capturing the total meaning of the man for rediscovery by endless generations of careful and sympathetic readers. He uses his diverse materials to articulate the main theme of the *Life:* the significance of Samuel Johnson's character as it emerges from the success story of his hardships and achievements. Although Boswell notoriously includes much seemingly irrelevant and rather recalcitrant trivia in Johnson's life story, he also frequently takes his reader's hand, helping him to discern behind the parade of ephemera the familiar and solid landscape of Johnson's personality. Boswell's guidance in these matters is conditioned by some of his specific attitudes toward Johnson and the *Life*.

When Boswell first met him in 1763, Johnson was fifty-four, with *The Rambler,* the *Dictionary, The Idler,* and *Rasselas* already behind him. Since Johnson's personality, like his reputation, had long since passed the early stages of development, it is not surprising that Boswell regarded him as a fixed entity, although at times a bewilderingly complex one: "At different times, he seemed a different man, in some respects; not, however, in any great or essential article, upon which he had fully employed his mind, and settled certain principles of duty, but only in his manners, and in the display of argument and fancy in his talk" (end of 1784). Thus the lack of development we see in Boswell's treatment of Johnson was in part built into the circumstances under which they knew each other. But there are two ways, probably related, in which Johnson himself is responsible for this stasis. First, his unusual integrity made him appear somewhat monolithic and unchanging. Second, his neoclassical stand on the uniformity of human nature—throughout the variety of one man's as well as of all men's acts—permanently influenced the young Boswell, who could see in himself only potentiality and flux.

In the opening pages of the *Life* Boswell observes that Johnson was remarkable from his earliest years and then uses part of Johnson's "Life of Sydenham" as if it were describing this uniformity:

> That the strength of his understanding, the accuracy of his discernment, and ardour of his curiosity, might have been remarked from his infancy, by a diligent observer, there is no reason to doubt. For, there is no instance of any man, whose history has been minutely related, that did not in every part of life discover the same proportion of intellectual vigour. [1712]

Shortly afterward, in telling us about Johnson's superiority among his schoolfellows, Boswell unwittingly transforms his subject into a faintly grotesque Johnsonunculus, rolling about among his little peers, offering them assistance with their studies and radiating intellectual excellence: "In short, he is a memorable instance of what has been often observed, that the boy is the man in miniature: and that the distinguishing characteristicks of each individual are the same, through the whole course of life" (1719–25). From the very beginning of the *Life* we find references to Johnson's fixed, though not necessarily consistent, qualities: his idleness, powerful memory, benevolence, humility, fear of death, curiosity, courage, kindness, respect for birth and rank, roughness, and love of good company. Johnson's personality is set out in a sprawling network of motifs whose recurrence establishes in the reader an almost real-life familiarity with the man and, Boswell hopes, some kind of sympathy for his opinions and daily problems.

The lack of character development in Boswell's history of Johnson is in keeping with popular English historiography before the nineteenth century. Assuming that the uniformity of human nature cuts across all barriers of time and culture, many historians viewed the past as only yesterday and ex-

amined the behavior of past figures as if they were Englishmen in a different setting. With his usual clarity, Swift expresses this view: "I cannot possibly see, in the common
Course of Things, how the same Causes can produce different Effects and Consequences among us, from what they did
in *Greece* and *Rome*."[3] In the eighteenth century, however,
the awakening of the historical sense truly began, as increasing attention was paid to the complementary concepts
of individuality and cultural development. The findings of
legions of investigators began to be consolidated, and anti-
quarianism gave way to a sounder historical perspective in
which human personalities and institutions were seen in
constant, complexly molded development rather than in
stasis or cycles or simplistic marches toward improvement.[4]

Despite the countless inconsistencies and contradictions in
historiography in this transitional period, however, the hero
of the *Life* has a static character. As the episodes and details
accumulate, Boswell holds Johnson up for our view and
slowly rotates him, like a huge cut gem, to display his many
facets. Since Johnson's brilliance, integrity, and inner doubts
are fixed qualities, our main interest is in the ways he over-
comes society and himself to make his way and to translate
this brilliance into lasting achievements. In addition to his

3. Swift, *A Discourse of the Contests and Dissensions between the
Nobles and the Commons in Athens and Rome;* quoted in Herbert
Davis, "The Augustan Conception of History," *Reason and the Imagination: Studies in the History of Ideas 1600–1800,* ed. J. A. Mazzeo, p. 226.
This matter is elaborated by James William Johnson in "Swift's Historical Outlook," *Journal of British Studies* 6, no. 2 (May 1965): 52–77:
Swift's strong belief in original sin and free will predisposed him to see
world history as an eternal cycle of man's aspiration to grace and his fall
from it. These cycles do not constitute an overall progression toward or
away from a golden age because man's spark of divinity and inherent tendency toward moral degeneration cancel each other out in the long run
of history.

4. See René Wellek, *The Rise of English Literary History.*

didactic motive for writing Johnson's biography, Boswell is also motivated by the desire to add Johnson's conversations to the number of these achievements. Even one who only browses through the *Life* must sense that the immediacy of these conversations somehow works against the static view of Johnson's character. This feeling may be substantiated by noting the effect of Boswell's two models for the *Life:* the traditional collections of ana, as modified by the new method of biography which grew out of his Journals; and a painting, a huge portrait of Johnson in which each new detail is another brushstroke. The first model is literary and temporal, whereas the second is plastic and spatial.

George Griffiths, a contemporary reviewer, first likened the *Life* to Xenophon's *Memorabilia* of Socrates and the "Books in Ana."[5] Griffiths also refers to the *Life* as a "voluminous journal." Because of Boswell's programmatic statements at the beginning of the *Life* and his numerous references to his Journals, any reader—especially one of Boswell's contemporaries—would see the biography as a hybrid outgrowth of the collection-journal traditions, in some ways like Mrs. Piozzi's *Anecdotes of Dr. Johnson.* Behind these seemingly compatible genres, however, there are opposing motivations: the collection, in particular the gossipy compilation in classical and French literature, was usually intended to demonstrate the fixed, though perhaps complicated, personality of an interesting figure. The journal, however, as originally written by the Puritans, was intended to trace for the benefit of its writer the ongoing war between good and evil in his soul. Even the slightest change of behavior or fortune was radically

5. *Monthly Review* 7 (Jan. 1792): 1; quoted in J. K. Spittal, *Contemporary Criticisms of Dr. Samuel Johnson, His Works and His Biographers*, p. 30. The reviewer is identified as George Griffiths by B. C. Nangle, *The Monthly Review, Second Series* (Oxford: Clarendon Press, 1955), pp. 26, 92.

important to the journal-keeper because it indicated his
progress toward or away from his eternal salvation.[6] The
journal served a similar purpose for Boswell, who used it as
"a faithful register of my variations of mind," a treasure to
be enjoyed many times afterward.[7] In Boswell's journal we
see the secularization of the Puritan practice: the journal has
become a part of his self-improvement program rather than a
spiritual record kept for religious purposes. The journal-
like nature of the *Life* consists in its attempt to put together
a connected narrative of Johnson's life story rather than a
description of only its highlights. But despite the parts of the
Life that march forward in a detailed chronicle of daily
living, despite Boswell's inclusion of Johnson's distraught
meditations on his backsliding, the *Life* is essentially a cele-
bration of Johnson's changelessness. Boswell's use of the
journal-collection as a model commits him to a detailed narration of actions, motives, and words, but not to a developmental view of character.

The other model for Boswell's biography is a large portrait
of Johnson like the one by Reynolds that the young Scot saw
before he met Johnson in 1763 and later received as a gift
from the artist.[8] In the dedication of the *Life,* addressed to
Reynolds, Boswell reveals that he has this portrait in mind:

> You, my dear Sir, studied him, and knew him well: you
> venerated and admired him. Yet, luminous as he was upon
> the whole, you perceived all the shades which mingled in

6. See William Haller, *The Rise of Puritanism*, pp. 96–100.

7. *Boswell on the Grand Tour: Germany and Switzerland, 1764,* ed.
Frederick A. Pottle, p. 58. Elsewhere, Johnson and Temple refer to
Boswell's Journals as a history, or record, of his mind.

8. Reynolds painted this portrait in 1756. It is sometimes called the
Boswell portrait because it was owned by Boswell and later inherited by
his son. Reynolds's four other Johnsonian portraits were painted after
1763 *(Life,* 4: 447–64).

the grand composition; all the little peculiarities and slight blemishes which marked the literary Colossus.[9]

Later, in the *Life* itself, Boswell uses this painting metaphor to justify his descriptions of Johnson's shortcomings:

And he will be seen as he really was; for I profess to write, not his panegyrick, which must be all praise, but his *Life;* which, great and good as he was, must not be supposed to be entirely perfect. To be as he was, is indeed subject of panegyrick enough to any man in this state of being; but in every picture there should be shade as well as light, and when I delineate him without reserve, I do what he himself recommended, both by his precept and his example. [Undated introduction]

I am fully aware how very obvious an occasion I here give for the sneering jocularity of such as have no relish of an exact likeness; which to render complete, he who draws it must not disdain the slightest strokes. [June 1764]

Boswell also uses this visual metaphor to head off the charge that a certain detail is too trivial; he defends it as "a small characteristick trait in the Flemish picture which I give of my friend, and in which, therefore, I mark the most minute particulars" (22 Sept. 1777). Here, "trait" probably has the additional force of "brushstroke," one of its French meanings. Not surprisingly, Boswell viewed his own past much as the historians of his age viewed man's collective past: history was a panorama of various scenes, figures, and settings—a

9. Robert E. Moore in "Reynolds and the Art of Characterization," emphasizes Reynolds's ability to combine type and individual in his portraits. He concludes: "He combined character with a certain sweetness, so that, while he is assuredly the greatest classical master of British portraiture, his appeal remains largely romantic. The sitter is there before us, but there is also something beyond, which is Reynolds himself" (p. 357).

series of still points. If one wants to capture the past in
words, even one's own past, one must anticipate some degree
of failure, Boswell says, for (and here he echoes Locke and
Hume) our ideas are based on our sense experience, which is
primarily pictorial:

> I observe continually how imperfectly, upon most occa-
> sions, words preserve our ideas. . . . All I have said of the
> Stratford Jubilee is very dim in comparison of the scene
> itself. In description we omit insensibly many little touches
> which give life to objects. With how small a speck does a
> painter give life to an eye![10]

If the past is a series of pictures, and writing a biography
the assembling of one big picture, then it is natural that
Boswell's main concern in composing the *Life* is striking the
proper balance between light and shade (virtues and vices)
rather than filling all the transitions between Johnson's important moments. Boswell's overwhelmingly detailed chronicle stems mainly from his desire to paint a portrait with
meticulous brushwork, not to provide us with a sequentially
complete record of Johnson's life.

It is significant that Boswell and Johnson liken the historian Dr. William Robertson to a painter because he imaginatively augments many of his scenes. Significant also is
Boswell's defense of this approach to history, which betrays
at an early date his preference for a dramatically heightened
(though historically faithful) scene to a combination of chro-
nologies and reconstructed third-person narrative.

> BOSWELL. "Will you not admit the superiority of Robert-
> son, in whose *History* we find such penetration—such
> painting? JOHNSON. "Sir, you must consider how that pene-

10. *Boswell in Search of a Wife, 1766–1769,* eds. Frank Brady and F. A.
Pottle, p. 292.

tration and that painting are employed. It iş not history, it is imagination. He who describes what he never saw, draws from fancy. Robertson paints minds as Sir Joshua paints faces in a history–piece: He imagines an heroic countenance. You must look upon Robertson's work as romance, and try it by that standard. History it is not." [30 April 1773][11]

Another metaphor implying Boswell's static view of Johnson and the *Life* may be found in the Advertisement to the first edition, in which he apologizes for the delay of the work's publication, explaining that it

must be imputed, in a considerable degree, to the extraordinary zeal which has been shewn by distinguished persons in all quarters to supply me with additional information concerning its illustrious subject; resembling in this the grateful tribes of ancient nations, of which every individual was eager to throw a stone upon the grave of a departed Hero, and thus to share in the pious office of erecting an honourable monument to his memory.[12]

The general impression of stasis in the *Life* is further reinforced by the very limited sections of connected narrative;

11. See also Johnson's remarks over six years later: "Robertson paints; but the misfortune is, you are sure he does not know the people whom he paints; so you cannot suppose a likeness. Characters should never be given by an historian unless he knew the people whom he describes, or copies from those who knew him" (10 Oct. 1779).

12. In a letter to William Bowles 14 June 1785, Boswell promises: "In the Great Literary Monument which I am ambitious to erect to the memory of our illustrious departed Friend, I wish that those who are able to bear an honourable part, should each have a pillar inscribed with his own name." Less than three weeks later on 1 July he writes to Joseph Cooper Walker: "It is my design in writing the Life of that Great and Good Man, to put as it were into a Mausoleum all of his precious remains that I can gather" (*Correspondence . . . Relating to the Making of The Life of Johnson,* ed. Marshall Waingrow, pp. 111–12).

the frequent mixing of time levels; Boswell's familiar complaints that he did not get all of a scene down, or that he
cannot remember it at all; his introductions to disconnected
Johnsonian conversation with words to the effect, "here are
the best parts, lumped together"; and his violations of chronology to juxtapose relevant material. Even the great dramatic scenes, such as the first meeting at Davies's shop and the
dinner at Dilly's, are exhibited as self-contained vignettes,
delicious things to be savored in themselves. Finally, the
organization of the *Life* until Boswell's meeting with Johnson necessarily emphasizes topics rather than chronology.
Much of this early section is little more than an examination
of Johnson's traits and an elaborate *catalogue raisonné* of
his works for each year (see Appendix I).

For all these reasons, Boswell's comparison of the *Life* to a
painting does seem apt. The relationship of its parts is much
more spatial (i.e., formed according to principles of relevance
and similarity rather than simple temporal contiguity) than
its chronological framework would at first suggest. Historically, the reason behind Boswell's readily choosing the painting metaphor is the venerable doctrine *ut pictura poesis,*
which blurred distinctions between the plastic arts and literature by advocating temporality (narrative) in painting and
sculpture, and spatiality in imaginative writing.[13] Deriving

13. The spatiality referred to here derives from the writer's organization of his material according to a static interpretation of reality (e.g.
Boswell's view of Johnson's character) rather than the simple sequence
of events as they actually happened. This is not to be confused with the
more radical "spatial form" which some works of modern literature
possess because their meaning is "reflexive," that is, constituted by the
relationship of their own parts to each other rather than the relationship
of their words to the external world; see Joseph Frank, "Spatial Form in
Modern Literature." Perhaps the ultimate distinction between these two
kinds of spatial form is only a matter of degree, depending on the extent
to which the artist has internalized his experience and shaped it with his

from Horace, the doctrine received wide support in eighteenth-century France, Germany, and England.[14] Boswell
was probably familiar with Dryden's elaborate "Parallel
between Poetry and Painting," the introduction to his translation of Du Fresnoy's *De Arte Graphica*. Undoubtedly
Boswell read the many *Spectator* papers in which Addison's
and Steele's belief in the doctrine quietly conditions their
aesthetic responses. Steele pleads for moralistic narrative in
painting: "I have very often lamented and hinted my Sorrow
in several Speculations, that the Art of Painting is made so
little Use of to the Improvement of our Manners."[15] Giving
further coherence to this position is Addison's series "On
the Pleasures of the Imagination" (nos. 411–421, June–July
1712), in which the wandering thread of his argument ultimately reveals its indebtedness to Lockean sensationalism as
he compares enjoying the products of our imaginations to

---

imagination; however, Boswell's *Life* is solidly in the mimetic tradition
of literature, while Frank's examples *(Ulysses, Nightwood,* and *A La
Recherche du Temps Perdu)* are in the modern, expressive tradition.

14. For a history of the doctrine, see Rensselaer W. Lee, *"Ut Pictura
Poesis,"* pp. 197–269; and Ralph Cohen, *The Art of Discrimination,*
pp. 188–247. The poetry-painting simile may be seen as one of the many
techniques used to demonstrate the unity of the arts. Although Lessing's
Laokoön (1766) reveals the inherent fallacy of the doctrine, his criticism
did little to discourage the ambitious unifiers. Boswell never read
Laokoön, nor, on his Grand Tour in Germany, did he meet Lessing, who
was in Breslau at the time. The importance of this doctrine in Reynolds's
Discourses has been examined by Harvey D. Goldstein in *"Ut Poesis
Pictura:* Reynolds on Imitation and Imagination," pp. 213–235. Goldstein
shows that, for Reynolds, the imagination is a gatherer of particulars
which it arranges so that it "unites thought and feeling and achieves for
mental qualities a proper sensory embodiment" (p. 233). Thus, Reynolds
sees that general ideas "involve neither vagueness nor cold abstraction,
but rather fullness and coherence" (p. 234). Since the products of the
imagination are an improvement over our imperfect world, they have a
timeless, static, universal significance.

15. *The Spectator,* ed. Donald F. Bond, vol. 2, no. 226, p. 378.

strolling through a picture gallery.[16] As used by the Augustan critics, the doctrine *ut pictura poesis* often implies a concern with a work's overall design or general meaning as opposed to its verbal details.[17]

In a basic, but vague and far from programmatic way, the doctrine seems also to have influenced Boswell, suggesting to him that his narrative could have a general unity despite its many parts and details of less than crucial relevance. In addition, the implications of *ut pictura poesis* contributed to Boswell's static view of Johnson by predisposing him to see his mentor as a fixed object to be represented pictorially. But this raises a problem. If Boswell arranges his materials according to a fixed view of Johnson, then what is the source of the *Life*'s undeniable vivacity, the feeling of lively motion that keeps the reader from nodding as he does in reading Hawkins's *Life*? Clearly it is not always the significance of the unchanging Johnson, nor the animation of his talk, nor the sometimes journal-like continuity of the *Life* that provides this interest. The answer lies in Boswell's narrative method: specifically, the way in which he mixes time levels and varies his distance from the historical moment.

16. "My Design being first of all to Discourse of those Primary Pleasures of the Imagination, which entirely proceed from such Objects as are before our Eyes; and in the next place to speak of those Secondary Pleasures of the Imagination which flow from the Ideas of visible Objects, when the Objects are not actually before the Eye, but are called up into our Memories, or formed into agreeable Visions of Things that are either absent or Fictitious" *(Spectator,* vol. 3, no. 411, p. 537).

17. William K. Wimsatt, Jr., and Cleanth Brooks, *Literary Criticism: A Short History,* p. 264n. The use of the painting metaphor to stress some kind of overall design in literature goes back to Aristotle: "The plot then is the first principle and as it were the soul of tragedy: character comes second. It is much the same also in painting; if a man smeared a canvas with the loveliest colours at random, it would not give as much pleasure as an outline in black and white" *(Poetics,* trans. W. H. Fyfe [Cambridge, Massachusetts: Harvard University Press, 1927], p. 27).

In his opening statement of purpose, Boswell acknowledges that he considers the particular value of the *Life* to be the large amount of Johnson's conversation in it. This virtue, of course, derives from his Journals, to which he often refers in the *Life*. A little over a year and a half before Johnson's death Boswell devoted a whole number of *The Hypochondriack* to diaries; here, he maintains that one can overcome the difficulty of keeping a journal only if "one has a peculiar talent for abridging":

> I have tried it in that way, when it has been my good fortune to live in a multiplicity of instructive and entertaining scenes, and I have thought my notes like portable soup, of which a little bit by being dissolved in water will make a good large dish; for their substance by being expanded in words would fill a volume.[18]

"Portable soup" is an apt metaphor. Soon after first meeting Johnson, Boswell became "strongly impregnated with the Johnsonian aether" and was able to expand his rough notes into extended conversation. This expansion could be done a few days after the fact, for his Journal, or over the distance of many years, as he did for portions of the *Life*. What made this process possible was Boswell's remarkable memory, which needed only the slight prodding of very sketchy notes to stimulate it into almost total recall.[19] Many remembered events could be vastly expanded, depending on the amount of treasured Johnsoniana they contained: indeed, an examination of Boswell's manuscript of the *Life* reveals that the large-scale changes, involving two or more sentences, are much oftener additions than excisions.

Even a cursory glance at the *Life* will reveal that there are

18. *The Hypochondriack,* ed. Margery Bailey, 2: 259.
19. Frederick A. Pottle, "The Power of Memory in Boswell and Scott," pp. 174–77.

periods which are covered in great detail, like the death of
Johnson's wife or Boswell's almost annual spring trips down
to London, followed by whole months which are glossed over
in a few sentences or omitted altogether. Obviously, Boswell's
many hurried transitions were forced upon him by his lack
of materials. But whatever the reason for these inequalities,
they help provide us with a sense of movement in the narrative; they help sustain our interest because they constitute
an ever-changing pace in the ongoing story of Johnson's
life.[20]

Several things affect a story's narrative pace; the term
"pace," in fact, may be defined objectively and subjectively.
In either case, it is a relative term whose meaning depends on
contrasts. Objectively, pace is determined by the rate of a
narrator's progress through the time-span that he has allotted
himself. For instance, a quick-paced detective thriller, *Rod-*

20. The theoretical basis for the following discussion of structure and
form in the *Life* comes from Monroe C. Beardsley's *Aesthetics: Problems
in The Philosophy of Criticism*. Since, for Beardsley, any verbal expression must have a structure, his concept of the term is rather austere.
There are two general kinds of structure, *perspectival* and *developmental*.
Perspectival structures are based on the "various possible relationships
between the speaker and his situation" (p. 247). These relationships are
spatial, which determines point of view, and *temporal*, which is created
by a work's prevailing tense, against which the writer, like Boswell, may
set contrasting time levels. These structures were discussed in my first
chapter. There are three developmental structures: *logical*, in which
sentences are linked by logical relationships such as cause and effect,
premise and conclusion, and so forth; *narrative*, which is the simple,
uninterpretative recording of action; and *dramatic*, which "consists of
variations in the on-goingness of the work, in its pace and momentum"
(p. 251). Beardsley associates this dramatic structure with the "kinetic
pattern" of music, which is the "pattern of variation in its propulsion,
or intensity of movement" (pp. 251, 184). The only two of these five
structures that are (theoretically) mutually exclusive are logical and
narrative, though in fact we everywhere see writing in which there is
an inextricable mixture of the observer's desire to record and his desire
to interpret what he sees in terms of logical categories. The whole *Life*,
in fact, is a tug-of-war between these two structures.

erick Random, or *Moll Flanders,* can all be read in far less time than their action covers, while parts of *The Faerie Queene, Tristram Shandy,* or *To The Lighthouse* have a much slower pace (objectively) because their reading time equals, or perhaps even exceeds, the time required for the external or mental action. An unflagging pace, fast or slow, is too much for most modern readers: fast-paced works may bore us because they have not revealed enough of their characters to convince us that we should be interested in them. This would be the case with most detective stories were it not that our main interest is the reconstruction of the crime from the available clues. The objective pace of the *Life* progressively slows down: a graph of the number of pages per yearly entry would look like an up-and-down stock market chart with the general trend upward and the final high point representing the tremendous section for Johnson's last year. This is a structural pattern that suggests not only the slow running down of the vast energy that had propelled Johnson through so much adversity but also his increasing acceptance by others as the great Cham of literature, the still point around which was organized the culture of an age.

But narrative pace also is established by certain more subjective elements in the reading experience, such as the relative speed and violence of both internal and external events. A reader will remain interested in a suddenly slower-paced narrative when the action is, say, Molly Seagrim's epic churchyard battle in *Tom Jones* or the Proudies' reception for the Stanhopes that becomes a drawing room apocalypse in *Barchester Towers.* Frequently, when the action itself accelerates, the writer's prose falls somewhat into associative rhythm, an essentially subliterary tempo dominated by the short and irregular phrase that has an ongoing momentum related to colloquial speech.[21] Since this kind of prose, which strives

21. Northrop Frye, *The Well-Tempered Critic,* pp. 55, 71, 81–82.

to become a continuous flow, reads faster than the discontinuous structures of more formal prose, the reader is, in a sense, compensated for the slower pace brought on by a crowding together of events in close sequence.

Thus, analogous to the oscillation of pace in the large-scale blocks of the *Life*'s narrative are the variations in our rate of reading Boswell's style. Actually he has three basic styles, each with its characteristic reading speed: the slow, ponderous, pseudo-Johnsonian moralizing and evaluating manner; the clearer, loosely subordinated, largely additive sentences of his narrative; and his rapid, realistic conversations. (It should be remembered, however, that Johnson, ever the conscious stylist, has the most formal and discontinuous speech of anyone in the *Life*.) In the world of the *Life*, the conversations are the most animated events we are privileged to witness; indeed, remembering Johnson's forensic belligerence, we may call some of these exchanges even violent.

Within a passage that reads at generally the same rate (moralizing-evaluative, narrative, or conversation) we can sometimes see Boswell's unusually keen appreciation for the contrast between long and short independent clauses quickening even his slower paragraphs with alternating rhythms. The following paragraph has been broken up to emphasize the varying lengths of each main clause with its subordinate elements. Since these sections are sense units as well as grammatical wholes, the divisions may not be universally acceptable, but the principle of contrast which they demonstrate remains clear and can be found at work in every part of the *Life*.

> While the world in general was filled with admiration of Johnson's *Lives of the Poets,* there were narrow circles in which prejudice and resentment were fostered, and from which attacks of different sorts issued against him.

By some violent Whigs he was arraigned of injustice to
Milton;

by some Cambridge men of depreciating Gray;

and his expressing with a dignified freedom what he
really thought of George, Lord Lyttelton, gave offence to
some of the friends of that nobleman, and particularly
produced a declaration of war against him from Mrs.
Montagu, the ingenious Essayist on Shakespeare, between
whom and his Lordship a commerce of reciprocal compliments had long been carried on.

In this war the smaller powers in alliance with him were
of course led to engage, at least in the defensive, and thus I
for one was excluded from the enjoyment of "A Feast of
Reason," such as Mr. Cumberland has described, with a
keen, yet just and delicate pen, in his *Observer*.

These minute inconveniencies gave not the least distur-
bance to Johnson.

He nobly said, when I talked to him of the feeble, though
shrill outcry which had been raised, "Sir, I considered myself as entrusted with a certain portion of truth.

I have given my opinion sincerely;

let them shew where they think me wrong." [Early 1781]

Occasionally Boswell abandons this principle of contrasting prose rhythms and sense unit lengths; instead, he delays
the climax of a sentence by various slight pauses and retards
so that the increasing tension dissolves only with the final
words.

At last, on Monday the 16th of May, when I was sitting in
Mr. Davies's back-parlour, after having drunk tea with him
and Mrs. Davies, Johnson unexpectedly came into the

shop; and Mr. Davies having perceived him through the glass-door in the room in which we were sitting, advancing toward us,—he announced his aweful approach to me, somewhat in the manner of an actor in the part of Horatio, when he addresses Hamlet on the appearance of his father's ghost, "Look, my Lord, it comes." [16 May 1763]

The corresponding sentence from the *London Journal* is the plainest possible narrative: "I drank tea at Davies's in Russell Street, and about seven came in the great Mr. Samuel Johnson, whom I have so long wished to see."[22] The suspense Boswell can generate may be dramatic, as above, or syntactic, as in the many periodic sentences that appear when he is writing on matters requiring judgment and philosophical detachment. Of course, both kinds of suspense usually exist together. The sentences below, from pages picked almost at random (dialogue passages were passed over because of the intrusion of Johnson's style), are periodic in varying degrees.

That Johnson had penetration enough to see, and seeing would not disguise the general misery of man in this state of being, may have given rise to the superficial notion of his being too stern a philosopher. [Mid 1750]

Yet, whatever additional shade his [Johnson's] own particular sensations may have thrown on his representation of life, attentive observation and close inquiry have convinced me, that there is too much of reality in the gloomy picture. [April 1759]

It has been suggested by some, with what truth I shall not take upon me to decide, that he rated the consequence of those islands [the Falklands] to Great-Britain too low. [Beginning 1771]

22. *London Journal, 1762–1763*, ed. Frederick A. Pottle, p. 260.

When he and I were one day endeavouring to ascertain, article by article, how one of our friends could possibly spend as much money in his family as he told us he did, she [Mrs. Thrale] interrupted us by a lively extravagant sally, on the expence of clothing his children, describing it in a very ludicrous and fanciful manner. [29 April 1776]

Yet, though Johnson had this habit in company [of speaking in a high style], when another mode was necessary, in order to investigate truth, he could descend to a language intelligible to the meanest capacity. [March–April 1783]

And, surely, when it is considered, that "amidst sickness and sorrow," he exerted his faculties in so many works for the benefit of mankind, and particularly that he atchieved the great and admirable DICTIONARY of our language, we must be astonished at his resolution. [End of 1784]

Because the periodic sentence was traditionally part of the moralist's manner, Boswell, remembering especially Addison and Johnson, sought to use it appropriately; in addition, his tendency to tease, however quietly, his expectant audience may be seen as part of his fine sense of dramatic values and of his flair for the dramatic gesture. When the verbal details, phrases and clauses of a sentence proliferate, postponing the resolution of the main clause, the last few words can achieve a dramatic climax ranging from the thundering finish of "Look, my Lord, it comes" to the satisfying completion of a thought.

A last, and extremely important, subjective determinant of narrative pace is the reader's awareness of the relevance of an event to a story's larger direction and plan; that is, when a reader senses that several plot-strands or themes are converging in one scene and that they are noticeably proceeding toward some resolution or end, then the details of that scene become intensely significant and even thrilling, and the pace picks up. In other words, narrative pace is determined by the writer's progress through the larger significance of his story's action (which may be symbolic, psychological, moralistic, and so on) as well as through the timespan that he has allotted himself. When days or even weeks of the *Life* open out into a wealth of conversations and circumstantial detail, the objective pace inevitably diminishes. To compensate for this, either the inherent liveliness of the action increases or Boswell halts the temporal progression of his story to draw a circle around an important event: By placing two or three observers on this circle, Boswell offers several points of view, a story in the round.

In the *Life* there are a few events which are neatly surrounded by a circle of observers. For the section covering the death of Mrs. Johnson, Boswell uses many materials because he is anxious to counter the popular notion that Johnson lacked any real affection for his wife. This section is a merry-go-round of emphases and perspectives: we have, in turn, Boswell's narrative, Johnson's prayer, excerpts from Johnson's *Prayers and Meditations* over the years, Mrs. Desmoulins's earlier report, Johnson's letter to Dr. Taylor, more Boswellian narrative, another of Johnson's prayers, Sir John Hawkins's account, another excerpt from the *Prayers and Meditations,* more Boswellian narrative, and finally Francis Barber's account. As a rule, Boswell fails to arrange so many materials around a static moment because he simply does not have enough documents. Some of his comments ("I love to exhibit sketches of my illustrious friend by various eminent hands") suggest that, if possible, he would have used relativistic narrative more often. The final sentence of the *Life* implies the importance of studying Johnson from as many viewpoints as possible: "Such a man was SAMUEL JOHNSON, a man whose talents, acquirements, and virtues, were so extraordinary, that the more his character is considered, the more he will be regarded by the present age, and by posterity, with admiration and reverence." From the early days of his *London Journal,* Boswell strongly associated Johnson's alluring complexity with London's, and, as Johnson himself observes, the tremendous multiplicity of London is such that it is many different things to different people (5 July 1763).[23] For Boswell, Johnson was a vast, significant, static entity who was perpetually, it seemed, surrounded by friends and admiring visitors. The sun-and-planets metaphor must have occurred to him more often than the one time he wrote to Johnson,

> My mind has been somewhat dark this summer. I have need of your warming and vivifying rays; and I hope I shall have them frequently. [August 1775]

Even the passage covering Mrs. Johnson's death, however, is not purely relativistic: there is considerable wavering in topic (Johnson's superstition is briefly treated) and time (Mrs. Desmoulins's report carries us up to the death). Elsewhere, when Boswell's materials for a period are especially scanty, they are strung together in chronological order, giving the reader a rather vague account of Johnson's linear progression through time. But as Boswell has at his disposal more and more information, he naturally uses it all and indulges his love for different views of Johnson. Much of the *Life* is written on this middle level, with too many materials for a simple linear story and not enough to encircle every important event with a gallery of observers. To examine the conse-

23. See also Johnson's remark to Boswell: "Why, Sir, I am a man of the world. I live in the world, and I take, in some degree, the colour of the world as it moves along" (14 July 1763). In addition, the theme of *Adventurer* no. 67 is the civilizing and therapeutic value of variety, especially that which a great metropolis can afford.

quences of this kind of narrative for the overall pattern of
the *Life* is to pass by gentle degrees from a consideration of
structure to one of form.[24]

Anyone who attempts to discuss the form of a digressive
work like the *Life*, especially one who is anxious to represent this form as a spatial model, had better remember the
fun Sterne had at the expense of those who might attempt to
diagram his deviations from the straight line of his plot.
Sterne confesses that in the first four books of *Tristram
Shandy* he has wandered shamelessly, and he draws four
squiggles to represent the pattern of each book. He boasts
that he has behaved much better in the fifth book, however:
he has broken down into only one real digression and several
parenthetical comments. This pattern is charted by a black
line that is relatively straight until the end, where it madly
darts out in a curlicue that vaguely resembles a G clef.[25] If
we keep this lesson of Sterne's in mind, we should retain
our critical humility while examining the implications of a
basic structural principle in eighteenth-century art and literature.

In *The Metamorphoses of the Circle*, Georges Poulet amas-
ses much evidence to demonstrate that the arts of the eigh-

24. This distinction between form and structure is based on that made
by Beardsley: structure is constituted by the "relatively large-scale relations among the main parts," "relations among large, and perhaps distant, regions," while "the form of an aesthetic object is the total web of
relation among its parts" (pp. 168–69). For Beardsley, structure necessarily
exists in any verbal expression (see n. 19), whereas form involves the
more intricate pattern of a work's smaller and larger parts, a pattern
which often is most conveniently represented by a spatial model. Such
models for form in literature may be found in Dorothy Van Ghent's
treatments of *Wuthering Heights* and *Pride and Prejudice* in *The
English Novel: Form and Function*. For a survey of the recent history of
the terms, see René Wellek's "Concepts of Form and Structure in
Twentieth-Century Criticism," pp. 1–11.

25. *Tristram Shandy*, ed. James A. Work, pp. 473–74.

teenth century abandoned the perfectly closed and rounded
circle to explore the aesthetic pleasure derived from "curves
which are engendered one from another, but of which not
one closes upon itself to imprison unity."[26] In his preface to
The Analysis of Beauty, William Hogarth explains that on
the 1745 frontispiece to his works he called the serpentine
line on the painter's pallet "The Line of Beauty" because
of the infinite variety of its parts. He cites no lesser authorities than Michelangelo, Rubens, and Raphael to establish
the venerability of this curve as a source of grace in the visual
arts. Later, in chapter five, Hogarth generalizes on the value
of variety and intricacy in our experience, including literature.

> Pursuing is the business of our lives; and even abstracted
> from any other view, gives pleasure. Every arising difficulty,
> that for a while attends and interrupts the pursuit, gives a
> sort of spring to the mind, enhances the pleasure, and
> makes what would else be toil and labour, become sport
> and recreation. . . . It is a pleasing labour of the mind to
> solve the most difficult problems; allegories and riddles,
> trifling as they are, afford the mind amusement: and with
> what delight does it follow the well-connected thread of a
> play, or novel, which ever increases as the plot thickens,
> and ends most pleas'd, when that is most distinctly un-
> ravell'd?[27]

26. Georges Poulet, *The Metamorphoses of the Circle,* trans. C. Dawson
and E. Coleman, p. 52.

27. William Hogarth, *The Analysis of Beauty, Written with a view of
fixing the fluctuating Ideas of Taste* [1753], ed. Joseph Burke, pp. 24–25.
On the title page is an epigraph from Milton: "So vary'd he, and of his
tortuous train / Curl'd many a wanton wreath, in sight of Eve, / To lure
her eye." Directly below this quotation is a design summarizing Hogarth's
argument: on top of an opaque horizontal slab labeled "VARIETY" rests
a transparent pyramid on (or in) which is a solid black S-curve that
seems to be a snake, with its relatively thick midsection, a tapering
"neck," and a head-shaped bulge at its upper tip.

The serpentine curve is the line of beauty for Sterne as well as for Hogarth. The wild flourish of Corporal Trim's cane (9. 4) drawn out on the page shows that the "line of beauty is thus also the line of liberty; in any case, of that liberty which consists in following one's own caprice, in adopting the changing itineraries which fancy proposes to the mind."[28] Summing up the implications of this line for eighteenth-century literature, Poulet draws some conclusions that, with a few changes, might be an analysis of the *Life*.

> The hero of the eighteenth-century novel, (up to Laclos) is not endowed with the faculty of arranging his life, or organizing his *self*. Both disappear in a jumble of lines so complicated that reason renounces deciphering anything, unless it be the extraordinary facility with which the mind can elude the very rules it has set itself.
>
> The construction of existence in the form of a sinuous line, therefore ends in failure, not from the non-obtaining of the objective, but by the absence of all objective. The sinuous line goes nowhere. It is a hieroglyph without signification, a scribble, a complicated but futile gesture. Unfaithful to the circle, erratic, supremely excentric, it becomes encumbered in its network, exhausts itself by the multiplicity of turns and returns, ends like a wearied river by dividing itself and becoming sluggish in some delta. A frequent happening in the eighteenth century is that of the exhaustion of caprice, the interruption of an activity which, from twisting and untwisting, tires of its spinning and stops no matter where.[29]

The serpentine line, then, is much more than a structural principle; it is one of the age's root metaphors, an analogue of mental activity and human behavior.

28. Poulet, p. 53.
29. Poulet, p. 54.

This sinuosity is the basic unit of form in the *Life*. One of the fundamental reasons for Boswell's inclusiveness is his uncertainty as to which details in Johnson's life story will be important in the eyes of posterity. His principle is: when in doubt, include. Not only radically incapable of organizing his own self, Boswell was also unsure of his ability to see the eternally significant outline of Johnson's story, so that he hesitated to call a certain detail irrelevant. But Poulet's remark about the aimlessness of the scribble does not apply to a biography like the *Life*, since, on the level of plot, it has to close with Johnson's death, and on the level of meaning, it has at least the unity of the man's personality and career. More importantly, mental or emotional capriciousness is not the spring that animates the sinuosity of the *Life*. It is the capriciousness in life itself that is partly responsible: if the *Life* twists and turns, it is because events happen that way. For instance: Johnson decides to compile a dictionary, he publishes the plan, he works on it for the next five years, he writes the famous letter to Chesterfield, eventually the work is published, Boswell examines its method and content, and it becomes the cornerstone of Johnson's reputation, to be referred to casually at various subsequent times with almost unanimous awe and praise.

But more significant are the undulations in the form of the *Life* that Boswell does not inherit from his subject. As Sterne himself confesses, the sinuosity of *Tristram Shandy* is the result of an unresolved conflict between wit and judgment, wit being the principle of disorder that judgment constantly must strive to rein in. In writing the *Life of Johnson*, however, Boswell had before him the natural waywardness of a human life, so that the principle of disorder was already built in, as it were. The problem was to get everything down and yet indicate the general meaning that resided in the mass of events. For example, after printing Johnson's letter to Macpherson, in which he boldly refuses to be intimidated by his threats, Boswell quickly lists six occasions on which Johnson displayed fearlessness of bodily harm (Feb. 1775). In this way, the serpentine form of the *Life* results not only from the inherently twisting nature of events but also from Boswell's attempts to indicate general meaning by cutting across space and time in his narrative. To put it briefly, the sinuosity of *Tristram Shandy* is caused by the welling up of a fertile wit that is irrepressible, while the undulating form of the *Life* is the cumulative result of Boswell's evaluation and judgment, his dogged attempts to explain, to group together relevant details, and to give us the widest possible perspective of Johnson.

Since the metaphor of the serpentine curve seems generally apt for the *Life* but perhaps rather vague in its specific applications, we might review the ways in which the *Life* appears to have a sinuous form. The first way, discussed at the end of chapter one, involves the reciprocal relationship between Boswell's materials and stances. Either narrative element can become the occasion for the other. The stance may come first. Accompanying Johnson on a visit to Derby in the autumn of 1777, Boswell muses on his keen pleasure in walking about in unfamiliar places. After stating that this feeling comes from "an immediate pleasure of novelty" although "there is a sameness every where upon the whole," Boswell gives Johnson's extemporaneous essay on the minute diversities in the manner of shaving a man's face (19 Sept. 1777). More often, Boswell's stance is in reaction to his materials, as in his evaluation of *Rasselas:* "Notwithstanding my high admiration of *Rasselas,* I will not maintain that the 'morbid melancholy' in Johnson's constitution may not, perhaps, have made life appear to him more insipid and unhappy than it generally is; for I am sure that he had less enjoyment from it than I have" (April 1759). Boswell goes on to temper the harshness of *Rasselas* with his own sage advice "learnt from a pretty hard course of experience." The constant shifting of Boswell's emphasis between his materials and his intrusions has many implications for the thematic development of the *Life,* some of which will be examined in the next chapter. Here it is important to notice that this reciprocal, or symbiotic (another metaphor), relationship between materials and stances may be thought to constitute a sinuous form, recalling Poulet's statement about "curves which are engendered one from another."

Another way in which the form of the *Life* resembles a sinuous curve is evident in the constantly varying narrative pace. Even the rate of change changes. The articulation of this form occurs as a result of what Beardsley calls "dramatic structure" and "kinetic pattern" (see chap. 2, note 20). As already noted, many of these accelerations and decelerations in pace were forced on Boswell by the limitations of his materials. That it was Boswell's recorded conversations with Johnson which most noticeably expanded the *Life* is indicated by the rough correlation between the length of each year's entry and the number of days Boswell mentions seeing Johnson during that period (see Appendix 2). The extreme frequency with which Johnson saw Boswell on his jaunts to London in the 1770s is an effective counter to those who claim that the two were only acquaintances. But the gaps that remain elsewhere in the record help create the always expanding and contracting narrative line. A sinuosity results from the main narrator's position as a limited observer, not from the existence of a major theme (such as wit versus judgment) that implies oscillation.

The third source of sinuous form in the *Life* is Boswell's relativistic narrative method. The eighteenth century, according to Poulet, was an age in which truth was investigated by the accumulation of a series of points of view, all valid and united under God's omniscience.[30] The scarcity of documents prevents Boswell from giving a completely relativistic account of each major event in Johnson's life; therefore, with regard to the basic time level of the narrative, the historical view of Johnson moves forward in time, often slowing down to allow for some degree of relativism. But since these circles are seldom closed as tightly as the one around the event of Mrs. Johnson's death, we have the narrative moment, trailing along with it as it progresses the arcs of various sizes which represent relativistic circles in different stages of incompletion. Again, we have a form reminiscent of Hogarth's line of beauty or the swirl of Corporal Trim's cane.

Since there is much overlapping in these explanations of sinuous form, they cannot be considered as descriptions of three logically separate dynamisms, or complexes of literary relationships. They are merely the three ways in which the mind most readily likens the development of the *Life* to a serpentine curve. What these three explanations have in common anticipates our discussion of Boswell's style: the sinuous form of the *Life* is a glistening pattern of temporal oscillations set in motion by a limited number of narrative devices that enable Boswell to alternate between a deep penetration of the historical moment and a distanced view of the action where commentary and interpretation are possible.

The strategy of this chapter has been to treat Samuel Johnson's character and life story as the main subject of Boswell's *Life*, and then to analyze the implications of this subject's development for the work's entire structure and form. Although the shape of this development has been emphasized rather than the nature of the man Johnson as he emerges in the *Life*, there is an aspect of the development which contributes

30. Poulet, p. 64.

to the static portrayal of Johnson's personality and facilitates Boswell's struggle to reveal the meaning in his story. At the very end of his study, Stauffer explains why the eighteenth century was the golden age of English biography:

> The classical and medieval theories of the stable social and religious order in which man was a subordinate part had not yet been completely supplanted by the introspective individualism of the Romantics. For a short period during this transition, man as an individual, and the world in which he lived, were both realities. Out of this fortunate moment, reflecting the interplay of old and new conceptions, rose the biographies of the eighteenth century in vigor and variety that have not been surpassed.[31]

This anticipates Poulet's remarks about the psychological relativism and perspectivism of the period.[32] We might expect in the *Life*, the shining product of this golden age, a picture of Johnson that is continuous from his innermost emotional life out to his externally visible social behavior. Instead, there is a gap in our knowledge that becomes more annoying and regrettable as we increasingly yield to the spell of the *Life* and muse on the man as a fascinating personality.

This continuity from the inner to the outer man is made up of several levels, or stages. First is the level of man's most private fears and goals. This is a landscape that has little connection with the external world, and it tends to be much the same in all men. For this reason, writing that describes, or comes directly out of, this inner world tends to be undiffer-

31. Donald A. Stauffer, *The Art of Biography in Eighteenth-Century England*, p. 553.

32. "The human being is a center toward which the outer reality converges and gets synthesized. Thanks to this organization, the outer is linked to the inner and the circumference to the center. The mind is capable of extending itself as far as the universe and the universe of converging upon the mind" (Poulet, p. 57).

entiated, repetitious, and, in large doses, dull. This is why most spiritual diaries and love letters make rather flat reading unless we know more about the people or situations. We have in the *Life* a sufficient selection from Johnson's *Prayers and Meditations,* some letters, and conversations to see him on this intimate level.

The next level of information is very poorly sketched out in the *Life.* It concerns the events that drive or shape one's emotional life permanently, the ways in which a man's personality arises and endures as he comes into contact with the outside world. (For reasons already noted, the eighteenth century would have said "endures" rather than "evolves.") This crucial part of our total knowledge of a man covers his progress into maturity, then the ongoing events that affect him most profoundly. If this information about Johnson was ever recorded, it was probably in the autobiographical material he burned a few days before he died. Boswell secretly read a good deal in these "two quarto volumes, containing a full, fair, and most particular account of his own life, from his earliest recollection" (early Dec. 1784), but he did not copy much from them.[33] Elsewhere, Johnson's temperament and sense of decorum predisposed him to speak in general terms of subjects that touched him to the quick. He was generally reluctant to discuss matters involving resolution and willpower: when Boswell asks him whether it is possible to "fortify our minds for the approach of death," he answers passionately, "No, Sir, let it alone" (26 Oct. 1769). Only in the last few years of his life, when he is dying, do his statements link this fear of death with specific parts of his experience:

> I have struggled through this year with so much infirmity of body, and such strong impressions of the fragility of life,

33. Of the few bits that Boswell copied from Johnson's journal, some were included in the *Life* and at least one was not. See Donald and Mary Hyde's "Dr. Johnson's Second Wife," pp. 133–51.

that death wherever it appears, fills me with melancholy; and I cannot hear without emotion, of the removal of any one, whom I have known, into another state. [7 Sept. 1782]

A dropsy gains ground upon me; my legs and thighs are very much swollen with water, which I should be content if I could keep there, but I am afraid that it will soon be higher. My nights are very sleepless and very tedious. And yet I am extremely afraid of dying. [11 Feb. 1784]

This balanced, connected view of Johnson's inner and outer worlds is rare in the *Life*. His fear of death is the only major topic treated in this way. Again, the gap can be explained in part by Boswell's lack of materials. Another explanation is Boswell's ambivalence toward introspection and detailed character analysis. Drawn as he was to the mysterious variety of the human personality, he realized that too close a look violated decorum and opened the way toward madness. The problems he encountered in his own self-investigations are the pathetic-comic background for the following pseudo-definitive solution to the problem, in which he is trying to convince himself as well as his audience:

For my own part, I look upon it as a great misfortune to be quick-sighted to the faults and imperfections of others. It is the great study of civilized life to promote good-humour and complacency, by making ourselves and every thing about us appear as agreeable as we can; for which reason we endeavour to keep out of sight whatever is imperfect and offensive; and our inventions are exercised in multiplying modes of cleanliness and ornament. *Swift* has shown us to a degree of exquisite disgust the consequence of prying, when we ought to be satisfied with external beauty of person and dress. If we will set ourselves to investigate in his manner, we all know what nauseous ideas will be excited; yet happily for us how very seldom are we disturbed by them as our views skim pleasingly along the surface. In the same manner we ought to conduct ourselves as to mental qualities; and not be always examining nicely into the characters of our neighbours.[34]

The last two levels of information about Johnson concern his external nature as a social being, and they are the meat of Boswell's biography. First are the attitudes and opinions, numerous and sometimes inconsistent, which are reconciled only by the psychological coherence of his personality. They are the reason for the extensive conversations. Then there are the man's appearance and his socially visible personality, that is, his behavior. This final level includes a man's ways of dealing with the external world, how he interacts with other people, and how he reacts to the problems that the world presents to him.

This gap in our knowledge of Johnson has important consequences for a reading of the *Life*. Perhaps the clearest one is the striking contrast between Johnson's *Prayers and Meditations* and his conversations caused by the lack of transitional material; indeed, Boswell tends to exploit this contrast by juxtaposing inner and outer views of Johnson to stress their difference more often than their similarity. More important and less obvious is the fact that, because the continuity in the description of Johnson is broken, and because the *Life* concentrates overwhelmingly on the external features of the man (the last two levels), Boswell often thinks of his work in terms of a flat space filled with the details that can be seen on the surface of Johnson's personality. In comparing his biography to a painted portrait, Boswell found a convenient and traditional metaphor for the situation. He often refers to the *Life* as a painting to suggest that he is including certain details even though they make impossible a

34. *The Hypochondriack,* ed. Margery Bailey, 1: 297.

soft-focus panegyric of Johnson or a logically consistent, generalized description of his character. Boswell tells us that he is including these maverick details because he wants to tell us the truth. To a modern reader this might seem to indicate the biographer's unwillingness to interpret his subject as he records it, but it was not until long after Boswell that the naturalistic implications of this metaphor were explored.[35] Boswell's work is still very much in the tradition of generalizing biography, and it has as its subject a man whose tremendous integrity makes him relatively easy to interpret. The inclusion of all doubtfully relevant details is based upon a mixture of humility and egoism. Who can say what is truly relevant? Boswell was sure that truth was a complex mystery whose outlines we may begin to discern only if we examine it from many perspectives and salvage as many pieces of the puzzle as we can. And yet, since the *Life* is partly his own story too, Boswell felt that some things should be in the portrait because they were important to him. Just as the presence of Reynolds's judgment and sensibility can be felt in his best portraits, so Boswell never lets us forget that he is not only Johnson's friend but also his biographer and the reader's guide.

35. Boswell's immediate effect on the history of English biography was to encourage even more authorial interpretation and intervention; see Francis R. Hart, "Boswell and the Romantics: A Chapter in the History of Biographical Theory," pp. 44–65.

CHAPTER THREE   *Boswell and*
His Journals:
"Let Us Live Double"

The *Life of Johnson* is notoriously a double portrait. As Boswell is filling in Johnson's features, he is also, through his literally thousands of authorial intrusions, sketching out a fair study of himself. In the dedication he makes the rather hurt announcement that his unguarded references to himself in the *Tour* as the butt of Johnson's satire have provided his enemies with ammunition, so that in the *Life* he has been careful to be more reserved. Fortunately for us, however, Boswell's censorship appears to have been minimal. Boswell's personality in the *Life* is essentially the one we find in the Private Papers: an unstable compound of sensitivity, callous pride, defensiveness, enthusiastic ingenuity, idealism, self-consciousness, and curiosity.

It is worth a brief digression from the *Life* to glance at an episode in Boswell's Journal that probably constitutes the best summary of his personality. This section covers the trial, conviction, and execution of John Reid for sheep-stealing, despite Boswell's defense of him in the face of overwhelming evidence. Although he originally planned to record the Reid affair only in his register of criminal trials, Boswell gives it an increasingly prominent place in his Journal from 1 August 1774 until the hanging on 21 September. In the *Life* he mentions Reid only once, in a short footnote. Boswell's defense is a thoroughly quixotic gesture, motivated by the combination of self-congratulation and compassion that ensued when, by court appointment, he successfully defended Reid as his first criminal client in 1766. Though the verdict is almost a foregone conclusion, the second trial is impressively dramatic: Boswell speaks before four unsympathetic judges of the High Court of Justiciary, two of whom are his own father and the redoubtable Henry Home, Lord Kames. After the defense can muster only one important witness to counter the compelling Lord Advocate and many crown witnesses, the jury retires and Boswell goes home to await the verdict. His reaction to the unfavorable decision involves a startling scene:

> Having heard that a verdict was found against John Reid, I went at eight to Walker's Tavern, where the jury were met (I having first visited my client and intimated his fate to him), and being elated with the admirable appearance which I had made in the court, I was in such a frame as to think myself an Edmund Burke—and a man who united pleasantry in conversation with abilities in business and powers as an orator. I enjoyed the applause which several individuals of the jury now gave me and the general attention with which I was treated. . . . we appointed to dine together in the same place that day sennight. There was a strange mixture of characters. I was not much pleased at being fixed for another meeting. However, I considered it as unavoidable, and as the buck in one of our farces says, 'twas *life*. We parted about twelve. I was in much liquor,

and strolled the streets a good while—a very bad habit which I have when intoxicated. I got home before one. My dear wife had been very anxious.[1]

The rest of Boswell's account up to the execution involves much unintentional comedy that is quite literally gallows humor. His egocentricity, his childish refusal to accept the cold verdict of the court, and his tactless curiosity concerning the condemned man's suffering are a kind of lightly moving counterpoint to the pathetic spectacle of the lower class Reid, who maintains his innocence yet submits meekly to his fate. When the "very curious whim" occurs to Boswell that he would like a portrait of his first criminal client, he hires a young painter, supposing that "John would have no objection, as it would not disturb him."[2] During the portrait sittings in prison, Boswell chats with Reid, their talk sometimes taking an almost unbearable turn:

> I spoke to him of his execution, thinking it humane to familiarize his mind to it. I asked him if he was here when Murdison died. He said no, and on my saying, "So you did not see him die," told me that he had never seen an execution. "No?" said I. "I wonder you never had the curiosity." He said he never had.[3]

Unknown to Reid and his wife, Boswell elaborately prepares to resuscitate the hanged corpse. A consultation with Dr. Alexander Monro convinces him that reviving a hanged man is possible by inserting a pipe through a hole in his trachea. For the operation, Boswell procures the proper equipment and a stable near the gallows. Boswell's long entry for 21 Sep-

1. *Boswell for the Defence, 1769–1774*, eds. William K. Wimsatt, Jr. and Frederick A. Pottle, pp. 252–53.
2. Ibid., pp. 283–84.
3. Ibid., p. 288.

tember recounts in sensitive detail the terrible last minutes
of Reid's life: the final words with his wife, the donning of his
white linen clothes and nightcap, and his forgiveness of the
hangman whose first task is to bind his elbows to his sides
with cord "to keep him from catching at the *tow*."[4] Outside,
the execution destroys Boswell's fantasy of resuscitating Reid:

> He was effectually hanged, the rope having fixed upon his
> neck very firmly, and he was allowed to hang near three
> quarters of an hour; so that any attempt to recover him
> would have been in vain. I comforted myself in thinking
> that by giving up the scheme I had avoided much anxiety
> and uneasiness.[5]

It is forever debatable whether Boswell is aware of his
failures in tact, taste, and sympathy in these scenes. The evidence appears to indicate that he is not. But, this matter
aside, Boswell's reactions to Reid's impending execution are
fragmented and varied. He lacks any fixed emotional attitude
to the situation: the gusto with which he arranges for the
resuscitation and pries into Reid's last-minute thoughts col-
lapses quickly into a genuine moroseness after the hanging.
He even extracts from Reid a promise to write a brief autobiography for him. Though Reid's execution affects him
deeply, so do all the others he ever sees; he is often morbidly
interested in hangings and condemned criminals because
they animate his already keen sense of mortality and his fear
of death.

In his Journals and in the *Life of Johnson,* Boswell reveals
the connection between his volatility and his self-centered-
ness. For most of his adult life he tried to puzzle out of his personal experience a rational pattern that he could call "James

4. Ibid., p. 331.
5. Ibid., p. 335.

Boswell."[6] He wanted this pattern to be both normative and descriptive. Significantly, it was his social behavior that most appalled him. In the *London Journal,* before he has met Johnson, he reveals that he has already diagnosed his problem shrewdly, but is not certain how to eliminate it:

> That is really a weakness about me, that I am easily overcome in any dispute, and even (as Dr. Brown has it) vanquished by a grin. . . . I am also much made by the company I keep. I should be very cautious in my choice. . . . Another shocking fault which I have is my sacrificing almost anything to a laugh, even myself; in so much that it is possible if one of these my companions should come in this moment, I might show them as matter of jocularity the preceding three or four pages, which contain the most sincere sentiments of my heart; and at these would we laugh most immoderately. This is indeed a fault in the highest degree to be lamented and to be guarded against.[7]

While studying law at Utrecht, Boswell draws up his formidable "Inviolable Plan," in which he admonishes himself to abandon his ways of idleness, dissipation, and spleen in order to follow a regular plan of living that will lead to a stable character, happiness, professional success, and eternal salvation. On the day that he drafts the plan, his Journal reveals a great determination to pull himself together:

> Read your Plan every morning regularly at breakfast, and when you travel, carry it in trunk. Get commonplace-book.

6. "No man ever watched with more pathetic eagerness for signs that the period of probation was over; no man ever felt a keener desire for improvement or a sharper need to be a person of steady consequence and solid worth. His radical uncertainty of his own identity made it enormously important to him to possess the respect and esteem of others" (Bertrand Bronson, "Boswell's Boswell," p. 69).

7. *London Journal, 1762–1763,* ed. Frederick A. Pottle, pp. 191–92.

Be one week without talking of self or repeating. The more and oftener restraints, the better. Be steady.[8]

Of course, this rehabilitation project was doomed from the beginning, just like many of his later literary projects.[9] As he confesses to Temple in a letter from Utrecht, "My misery is that, like my friend Dempster, I am convinced by the last book which I have read."[10] Almost a year later, while in Germany, Boswell's resolution reaches another high-water mark, when he sees that his chief error has been "in suffering so much from the contemplation of others":

I recollected my moments of despair when I did not value myself at sixpence, because, forsooth, I was but an individual, and an individual is nothing in the multitude of beings. Whereas I am all to myself. I have but one existence. If it is a mad one, I cannot help it. I must do my best.[11]

Boswell never fought free of his tendency to be "much

8. *Boswell in Holland, 1763–1764,* ed. Frederick A. Pottle, p. 47.

9. In *The Literary Career of James Boswell Esq.*, pp. 301–09, Pottle lists thirty-four "Projected Works," including a "Dictionary of Words peculiar to Scotland," an "Essay on the Genius and Writings of Dr. Young," "A History of Sweden," "A History of James IV of Scotland," "A Novel on Sir Alexander Macdonald," "A Life of Lord Kames," "An Edition of Izaak Walton's *Lives,*" "A Translation of Erasmus's *De Praeparatione ad Mortem,*" "Memoirs of David Hume," "A Collection of Feudal Tenures and Charters of Scotland," "An Edition of Johnson's Poems," "A Life of Sir Joshua Reynolds," "A Study of the Controversy over *The Beggar's Opera,*" and "A Reply to Dr. Parr and other Critics of *The Life of Johnson.*"

10. *Boswell in Holland,* p. 252.

11. *Boswell on the Grand Tour: Germany and Switzerland, 1764,* ed. Frederick A. Pottle, pp. 53–54. Boswell's backsliding in this matter was almost immediate. See his distressed letter written in French in July 1765 to Alexandre Deleyre, in *Boswell on the Grand Tour: Italy, Corsica and France, 1765–1766,* eds. Frank Brady and Frederick A. Pottle, pp. 105–06.

made" by the company he kept. It had its advantages: he was, as Johnson remarked, thoroughly "unscottified." And during a meeting in 1772 with the other partners in *The London Magazine,* he prides himself on being able to pass for an Englishman through his "perfect art of melting myself into the general mass"; however, he defensively adds, "when the heat is over, I gather myself up firm as ever, with perhaps only a small plate or thin leaf of the other metal upon me sufficient to make me glitter, and even that I can rub off if I choose it."[12]

Boswell's self-consciousness makes him an insatiable student of his own fluctuating behavior, ever on the alert lest the enduring pattern, his true self, escape unnoticed. Often he accepts ready-made models from real life, such as Steele, Johnson, or his father. In the early years, many of these models come from literature: Mr. Spectator, Hamlet, and Macheath. The dominant model of the *London Journal* is Macheath, as embodied in West Digges, Boswell's friend and one of the best players of the highwayman in all Britain.[13] Although Boswell kept his habit of using literary allusions to grace his Journal, after his Grand Tour he at least stopped searching in literature for his identity—a limited emancipation.

12. *Boswell for the Defence,* p. 100.

13. Johnston and Temple are two other real-life models for Boswell. Cf. R. S. Walker's observation: "The 'antisyzygy' of the post-Union Scot, as familiar today as in Boswell's day, is nowhere more vividly exemplified than by Boswell's conflicting selves—the one so deeply attached to the past, to Johnston, and to home; the other reaching out to Temple and aspiring to some higher and larger self-realization. Boswell seems to have thought of his friends as like the two sides of his nature, antipathetic to each other" (*The Correspondence of James Boswell and John Johnston of Grange,* ed. R. S. Walker, p. xviii).

For a survey of some of the literary models, see Paul Fussell, Jr., "The Force of Literary Memory in Boswell's *London Journal,*" pp. 351–57, and A. J. Tillinghast, "Boswell Playing a Part," pp. 86–97. Pottle mentions the Digges-Macheath model in *James Boswell: The Earlier Years, 1740–1769,* pp. 38, 96, 262.

Boswell's reason for keeping a journal is much like his aim in writing the *Life of Johnson:* both ventures try to strike a balance between the gathering of material and the expression of its general significance. Emphasizing the importance of details, Johnson gives Boswell advice on keeping a journal— advice that he himself could never follow:

> The great thing to be recorded, (said he,) is the state of your own mind; and you should write down everything that you remember, for you cannot judge at first what is good or bad; and write immediately while the impression is fresh, for it will not be the same a week afterwards. [11 April 1773]

Indeed, the two men had already found themselves in solid agreement about ten years earlier, when Johnson admonished Boswell to keep a detailed journal, and Boswell happily replied that he had been writing one for some time. When Boswell expressed the fear that some of the incidents in his Journal were too trivial, Johnson countered with his famous assurance, "There is nothing, Sir, too little for so little a creature as man" (14 July 1763).

In Boswell's Journal we have the spectacle of a man looking inward toward himself, enjoying with his audience the theater of his own mind.[14] Often he writes his Journal with a specific audience in mind. The *London Journal* was posted to his old friend Johnston in weekly installments of six quarto sheets. With an ingratiating blend of exhibitionism and warm friendship, Boswell expresses his driving desire to entertain and communicate:

> As you walk up the Canongate so called *a Cannonicis,* from the old monks, comfort yourself with thinking "I get a Packet of Journal to-night" and be pleased with your entire ignorance of what it will contain. Keep yourself in this

14. See Martin Price, *To the Palace of Wisdom,* pp. 343–45.

fine frame till night and then you will read it with such pleasure that you will think your existence worth enjoying tho' it were for no other end. Thus my freind have I poured forth my genuine feelings to you. I hope you will like them.[15]

Later, on his Grand Tour, he promises Temple that he will be "much entertained" by his Journal:

I will never disguise my fluctuations of sentiment. I will freely own to you my wildest inconsistencies.[16]

Boswell's purpose in recording all this variety is to discover in himself a fixed personality capable of being described by moral universals. That this should be the end of any life record was brought home to him by Johnson, whose biographies, such as *The Lives of the Poets,* added "philosophical research" to the ancients' "minute selection of characteristical circumstances" (beginning 1754). Further reinforcing Boswell's desire to see the general among the particulars in his and Johnson's life stories is his sensitivity to dramatic effects, to the overall impression made by a person, or the dominant mood of a scene. The following rather curious passage indicates his tendency to extract from the details of an episode the general atmosphere or "idea," the latter being a Humean construct based on sense experience and very directly related to his emotional life:

I must observe that my journal serves me not so much as a history as it serves me merely as a reservoir of ideas. According to the humour which I am in when I read it, I judge of my past adventures, and not from what is really recorded. If I am in gay spirits, I read an account of so much

15. *Correspondence of Boswell and John Johnston,* p. 50.
16. *Boswell in Holland,* p. 252.

existence, and I think, "Sure I have been very happy." If I am gloomy, I think, "Sure I have passed much uneasy time, or at best, much insipid time." Thus I think without regard to the real fact as written.[17]

Since Boswell's extraordinary memory and childlike curiosity led him to write an extremely full Journal, he was forever in danger of falling far behind. While young, he stays awake through many nights to catch up his Journal; as he grows older and more melancholic, the record often remains in the rough-note stage or breaks off altogether. Throughout his life, however, the Journal remains an obsession, and the further he falls behind, the more "hypped" he becomes. Having promised to send the weekly packets of his *London Journal* to Johnston by the Tuesday post, Boswell is startled one Tuesday to discover that he has nothing to mail; he dashes in confusion to his chambers and writes away as if his life depended on it.[18] More than ten years later, this compulsion has become less frantic, modulated into the almost heroic melancholy of a man who sees himself driven to attempt an impossible task:

> I am fallen sadly behind in my journal. I should live no more than I can record, as one should not have more corn growing than one can get in. There is a waste of good if it be not preserved. And yet perhaps if it serve the purpose of immediate felicity, that is enough. The world would not hold pictures of all the pretty women who have lived in it and gladdened mankind; nor would it hold a register of all the agreeable conversations which have passed. But I mean

17. *Tour: Germany and Switzerland*, pp. 143–44.
18. *Correspondence of Boswell and John Johnston*, p. 105. Boswell complains at one point: "I sat up all last night writing letters and bringing up my lagging journal, which like a stone to be rolled up a hill, must be kept constantly going" (*London Journal, 1762–1763*, p. 324).

only to record what is excellent; and let me rejoice when I
can find abundance of that.[19]

This is the source of the predominantly elegiac tone of the
Life. Boswell wishes to preserve the good in Johnson, who,
more than most men, grew more than anyone could gather
in. Ultimately, Boswell stands helpless before his project of
writing the *Life*, just as Johnson stood before his Dictionary
when he saw that his early ambitious plans "were the dreams
of a poet doomed at last to wake a lexicographer." In both
men this sense of inadequacy stems from their failure to describe fully the innumerable products of time, be they a
man's daily behavior or the changes in a living language.
Matters are further complicated by the fact that both men
regard the description of these processes of change as a glori-
ous and heroic achievement. For Johnson in his Dictionary
and Boswell in his Journal and the *Life*, allowing matter to
slip by unrecorded is a melancholy reminder of their frailty,
just like the countless backslidings after solemnly declared
resolutions against dissipation and whoring (Boswell) or
despair and indolence (Johnson). In both men these distresses
over each real or imagined failure mutually reinforce, blend,
spiral. All the flashes of pleasure and glee in the *Life* are only
momentary reprieves from the dark pain of existence.[20]

19. *Boswell: The Ominous Years, 1774–1776*, eds. Charles Ryskamp and
Frederick A. Pottle, p. 265. There is a similar passage in *Boswell in Search
of a Wife, 1766–1769*, eds. Frank Brady and Frederick A. Pottle, p. 242:
"I find it impossible to put upon paper an exact journal of the life of
man. External circumstances may be marked. But the variations within,
the workings of reason and passion, and, what perhaps influence happiness most, the colourings of fancy, are too fleeting to be recorded. In
short, so it is that I defy any man to write down anything like a perfect
account of what he has been conscious during one day of his life, if in any
degree of spirits. However, what I put down has so far an effect that I
can, by reading my Journal, recall a good deal of my life."
20. While laboring on his long-delayed biography of Johnson, Boswell
wrote to his old friend Temple: "Such is the gloomy *ground* of my mind,

Boswell's Private Papers suggest how his lack of a solid personal identity helps to generate the rapid oscillation of authorial stances and contributes to his own hypochondria and the melancholy tone of the *Life*. A closer look at these papers also reveals the peculiar theatricality of Boswell's personality, his strong predilection for the dialogue form, and his need to include himself in Johnson's life story.

Boswell's love of the theater goes back to his early days in Edinburgh, when he frequented the theater in the Canongate, revelled in the slightly wicked company of actors and actresses, and spun fantasies about being a dramatic critic, a playwright, and a patron. These experiences and the avid playgoing recorded in the *London Journal* doubtless increased the self-consciousness of the sensitive boy, making him aware of the roles men choose or have forced upon them in real life. Over the years Boswell's play-going and journal-keeping helped blur for him the distinction between art and life. Occasionally events seemed to conspire to make this confusion almost unavoidable, as when "Louisa" (Anne Lewis), a recent Gertrude in a Covent Garden *Hamlet,* played the surprised wounded party to his version of the reproachful prince. The dynamics of Boswell's awareness can be extremely complicated: in his Journal he is usually a faithful observer and a mercurial participant, with each half only minimally influencing the other. This split is largely responsible for Boswell's candor in his Journal, the *Tour,* and the *Life.*[21]

Another result of this split is that Boswell often casts his writing in the form of obvious or covert dialogues. Some of the French themes he wrote in Holland make use of an imag-

---

that any agreable perceptions have an uncommon though but a momentary brightness. . . . " *(Correspondence . . . Relating to The Making of the Life of Johnson,* ed. Marshall Waingrow, p. 291).

21. See Bronson, "Boswell's Boswell," pp. 64–65.

inary interlocutor, as when he congratulates himself on the calmness with which he has taken some impertinence from his servant:

> I take credit to myself for having been so reasonable with my servant in a situation where passionate people like yourself would have beaten him. You say to me, "Why not strike a servant sometimes, when one feels like it? It is an amusement of a sort, it relieves one's spleen to punish the cause of it. The desire to avenge ourselves on those who have offended us is universal; and Nature herself shows us that it is right. . . . " Sir, I must reply to your lesson in philosophy, but do not expect a word-for-word reply. Be content, Sir, if I refute you in the large.[22]

It becomes Boswell's habit to discuss matters dramatically, by voicing both sides in a debate.

> At night indolence made me think, why give myself so much labour to write this journal, in which I really do not insert much that can be called useful? Beg your pardon. Does it not contain a faithful register of my variations of mind? Does it not contain many ingenious observations and pleasing strokes which can afterwards be enlarged? Well, but I may die. True, but I may live; and what a rich treasure for my after days will be this my journal.[23]

A man who talks to himself like this need exert little effort to capture the lively rhythm of the following interchange:

> Of our friend, Goldsmith, he said, "Sir, he is so much afraid of being unnoticed, that he often talks merely lest you should forget that he is in the company." BOSWELL.

22. *Boswell in Holland*, p. 134 (translations by Pottle). See also pp. 48, 79.
23. *Tour: Germany and Switzerland*, p. 58.

"Yes, he stands forward." JOHNSON. "True, Sir; but if a man is to stand forward, he should wish to do it not in an aukward posture, not in rags, not so as that he shall only be exposed to ridicule." BOSWELL. "For my part, I like very well to hear honest Goldsmith talk away carelessly." JOHNSON. "Why yes, Sir; but he should not like to hear himself." [11 April 1772]

It is not surprising that Boswell was charmed by the energy of aimless, even inane, conversations and felt compelled to record many of them: witness his early dialogues at Child's and dialogues at The Hague. His fondness for the zigzag logic of a conversation can be seen even in the structure of his sentences using adversative conjunctions and phrases, a stylistic matter that will be discussed more fully in the next chapter.

Boswell's ability to reproduce the rhythm of give-and-take in a conversation naturally is such that the wit-combats in the *Life* evoke fully realized scenes. This effect is heightened when he writes dialogue in play form, using dramatic tags and stage directions like "laughing vociferously," "looking to his Lordship with an arch smile," or "much agitated." Johnson's statements are less dramatic when they are isolated and grouped together, but even these passages create a con- siderable dramatic illusion due to Boswell's sensitivity to Johnson's stylistic peculiarities, especially to the rhythm of his speech. Quite early in the *Life* we are given an elaborate description of the tics, tremors, whistles, and cluckings that accompany Johnson's talk (late 1764); later, Boswell urges us to "keep in mind his deliberate and strong utterance," which Lord Pembroke once referred to as Johnson's "bow-wow way," a characterization that appears first in the *Tour to the Hebrides* (entry for 1773) and later in the *Life* (note to 27 March 1775). Boswell demonstrates his sensitivity to the peculiar rise and fall of Johnson's voice when he laments the absence of someone to transcribe his speech by means of the new musical notation of Joshua Steele, who had worked on Garrick's recitations (27 March 1775).

When we look at the *Life* as a whole, we become aware of how often Boswell creates a dramatic illusion simply by appealing to our ears rather than to our eyes. Indeed, he confesses that Johnson, despite his poor eyesight, could describe external objects much better than he: "I said, the difference between us in this respect was that between a man who has a bad instrument, but plays well on it, and a man who has a good instrument, on which he can play very imperfectly" (22 Sept. 1777).[24] To be sure, there are descriptive passages in the *Life* that are sharp and economical. The slovenly Johnson in his chambers and his bizarre mannerisms while talking are scenes so vivid that they persist in our imagination throughout the *Life;* once established, they need not be recreated when the situation is appropriate. Like the stage directions in the *Life's* recorded dialogues, these scenes are a kind of dramatic shorthand. There are other vivid scenes, usually brief, such as Boswell and Johnson rowing serenely along the Thames (30 July 1763); Johnson bending over to encourage a little printer's apprentice with a guinea (27 March 1775); Johnson stirring up swirls of dust as he puts his books in order (3 April 1776); and Johnson using a long pole to clear Dr. Taylor's artificial waterfall of branches, rubbish, and a dead cat (22 Sept. 1777). But these visual scenes are as remarkable for their rarity as for their sureness of touch. Because he seems to have underestimated his ability to describe objects, Boswell's *Life* (much more than the *Tour)* does not display the sustained effort of a visual imagination

24. See W. K. Wimsatt, Jr., "The Fact Imagined," pp. 168–69.

that we find in *Pamela* or *Clarissa*.[25] The similarity between Richardsonian "writing to the moment" and Boswellian narrative (especially that in the Journals) derives from a common method rather than from Boswell's attempt to mimic the verbal details of Richardson's style; that is, both men were trying to catch in words the rhythm and associativeness of thought and conversation. To be sure, Boswell's familiarity with Richardson's successes reinforced his own confidence in following this method as a young writer.

There would seem to be a problem here. How is it that we remember the *Life* as a series of vivid scenes when in fact only a small fraction of it contains fully realized scenes which describe the actors and their setting? A partial answer is that Boswell enlists the imaginations of his readers to augment his brief hints of external detail.[26] He does this by communicating emotions to us so directly and convincingly that we accept them without reservation; then, we momentarily identify with the character, making ourselves at home by adding as much background and sensuous detail as we want. The emotions in question may be Boswell's, Johnson's or anyone else's, but they are almost always revealed in the act of speech, even if it is not quoted directly.

Johnson was in high spirits this evening at the club, and talked with great animation and success. He attacked Swift, as he used to do upon all occasions. The *Tale of a Tub* is

25. See George Sherburn's "Writings to the Moment: One Aspect," pp. 208–9. In "Boswell's Boswell," Bronson notes Boswell's visual imagination (pp. 91–92). While not denying that Boswell had this quality when he wanted to make use of it, we can still say that visual descriptions are not characteristic of the *Life*. Most of Bronson's examples are from the *Tour*, in which Boswell concentrates on the picturesqueness about him for the benefit of his English audience.

26. This explanation follows Wimsatt's in "The Fact Imagined."

so much superior to his other writings, that one can hardly believe he was the authour of it. "There is in it such a vigour of mind, such a swarm of thoughts, so much of nature, and art, and life." I wondered to hear him say of *Gulliver's Travels,* "When once you have thought of big men and little men, it is very easy to do all the rest." I endeavoured to make a stand for Swift, and tried to rouse those who were much more able to defend him; but in vain. [24 March 1775]

The clash of Johnson's overbearing bow-wow with Boswell's animated, abortive rally to Swift's defense can be heard clearly. Their talk is the important thing; each reader can paint in the scene with the background and furniture of his choice. This technique, too, is a kind of shorthand, a moderately diluted serving of portable soup that can be diluted still more. One need only read Balzac's lengthy description of the interior of Mme. Vauquer's boardinghouse in *Le Père Goriot* to see how much a writer can dilute a scene by attempting a detailed visual realization of a setting before he places his characters in it.

The most memorable narrative in the Journals fuses spare external description with Boswell's intense emotional reactions. Events become even more vivid when Boswell strictly limits his reactions to those of the moment, as when he preserves the delicious suspense in the Louisa episode even though, at the time of writing, the signs of gonorrhea were already unmistakable and the confrontation scene had occurred.[27] In the *Life* the liveliest narrative always covers the scenes in which Boswell is present as a kind of Jamesian reflector. Using an almost standard sentence structure to herald his spring arrival in London, Boswell quickens his narrative as he once again enters Johnson's life:

27. See *Correspondence of Boswell and John Johnston,* p. 42n.

On Tuesday, March 21 [1775], I arrived in London; and
on repairing to Dr. Johnson's before dinner, found him in
his study, sitting with Mr. Peter Garrick, the elder brother
of David, strongly resembling him in countenance and
voice, but of more sedate and placid manners.

On Monday, March 19 [1781], I arrived in London, and
on Tuesday, the 20th, met him in Fleet-street, walking, or
rather indeed moving along.... 28

If Johnson's life, character, and opinions constitute the
main subject of the *Life,* then the most important secondary
subject of the work is the friendship of Boswell and Johnson
over the years. This friendship was based on similar interests
and mutual needs. Both men highly respected rank and the
principle of subordination, and both were uncommonly animated by good company and sprightly conversation. They
were both subject to spells of melancholia, brought on by
their soul-wasting indolence and fear of death. Boswell found
comfort in Johnson as a source of parental authority and
affection—a father figure—while Johnson's attachment to
Boswell was, perhaps, more complicated. He saw himself in
the young Scot trying to make his way in London, his instincts
as a true teacher told him that here was someone who des-
perately needed guidance, he delighted in Boswell's unflinch-
ing candor, and he admired him as the heir of Auchinleck's
feudal privileges, a position that he, the son of a bookseller,
must naturally respect. In the *Life,* all of Boswell's recorded
conversations and his correspondence with Johnson contribute to this theme. Their friendship is not simply part of the
plot and action of the book; insofar as Johnson the man at-

28. See also 26 March 1768, 21 March 1772, 15 March 1776, 18 March
1778, 16 March 1779, 21 March 1783, 5 May 1784.

tains a general significance, his relationship with Boswell helps define that higher meaning.

In a number of places Boswell implies that he considers this friendship a static part of his experience. It is a thing, an object to be possessed; it is acquired, and then it is lost. This is the way Boswell sets the stage for 1763, his *annus mirabilis:* "This is to me a memorable year; for in it I had the happiness to obtain the acquaintance of that extraordinary man whose memoirs I am now writing; an acquaintance which I shall ever esteem as one of the most fortunate circumstances in my life" (beginning 1763). In similar terms, Johnson assures Boswell that the lag in their correspondence does not indicate any cooling off of their friendship: "I consider your friendship as a possession, which I intend to hold till you take it from me, and to lament if ever by my fault I should lose it" (23 Dec. 1775). Arriving in London one spring, Boswell seeks out Johnson and finds him at the Thrales's. In moments, he is basking once again in Johnsonian conversation: "I felt myself elevated as if brought into another state of being" (16 March 1776). This is revealing; in these later years, Boswell looked forward to his times with Johnson as a bracing tonic to his domestic and professional life in Scotland. Given his essentially fixed view of Johnson's character, it is not surprising that Boswell also saw their friendship in fixed terms. The reader's sense of this stability is reinforced by Boswell's many statements like, "during all the course of my long intimacy with him, my respectful attention never abated, and my wish to hear him was such, that I constantly watched every dawning of communication from that great and illuminated mind" (14 April 1775).

No faithful and detailed account of a long friendship, however, can sustain a note of such fixed, unbroken good will and understanding. Out of Boswell's Journals and letters come reports of setbacks as well as progress in the relationship. It was inevitable that two sensitive men who enjoyed lively repartee so immensely would annoy each other at times. More than once Boswell's pro-American sentiments annoyed Johnson. Boswell's defense of America's right of self-taxation forces his early departure from Johnson's apartment one evening (23 Sept. 1777). Less than a year later, Boswell again makes a similar defense in the presence of Johnson, who fumes silently. Minutes afterward, the topic having changed, Boswell speaks up and Johnson bludgeons him with a heavy insult. Shocked, Boswell asks him later in private why he was so harsh:

> JOHNSON. "Because, Sir, you made me angry about the Americans." BOSWELL. "But why did you not take your revenge directly?" JOHNSON. (smiling,) "Because, Sir, I had nothing ready. A man cannot strike till he has his weapons." This was a candid and pleasant confession. [18 April 1778]

Often the clash results from Boswell's excessively prodding questions. Buckling under the onslaught of Boswell's curiosity, Johnson would sometimes fight back:

> I will not be put to the *question*. Don't you consider, Sir, that these are not the manners of a gentleman? I will not be baited with *what,* and *why;* what is this? what is that? why is a cow's tail long? why is a fox's tail bushy? [10 April 1778][29]

Flying in the face of Johnson's certain anger one evening,

29. "Being irritated by hearing a gentleman [Boswell] ask Mr. Levett a variety of questions concerning him, when he was sitting by, he broke out, 'Sir, you have but two topicks, yourself and me. I am sick of both.' 'A man, (said he,) should not talk of himself, nor much of any particular person. He should take care not to be a proverb; and, therefore, should avoid having any one topick of which people can say, 'We shall hear him upon it' " (early May 1776).

Boswell pries into Johnson's fear of death and provokes a final "Give us no more of this" and "Don't let us meet tomorrow" (26 Oct. 1769). In the morning he sends Johnson a note of half-apology and half-complaint, saying that he will call on him that day as usual. On entering Johnson's study, Boswell sees that Mr. Steevens and Mr. Tyers are also paying a visit. After a while Boswell discerns that Johnson has probably been softened by his note, and, when the two others start to leave, Boswell moves to join them. Johnson bids him stay with "Get you gone *in*" (27 Oct. 1769). Directly addressing his readers, Boswell holds up "this little incidental quarrel and reconciliation" as evidence of Johnson's basic good humor. This is like the passage in which he maintains that Johnson's early kindnesses to him in 1763 refute the popular charge of harshness levied against him.

These reconciliations usually involve a renewed or increased understanding between the two men. When Johnson explains his unreasonable treatment of Boswell with "A man cannot strike till he has his weapons," Boswell is appeased, even charmed, because of his insatiable curiosity about Johnson's idiosyncrasies. If he were not so curious, he might have replied to Johnson that his explanation was no explanation at all. A similar conflict with a similar resolution arises during dinner with Reynolds, when, in front of many strangers, Johnson gruffly attacks Boswell. His pride is so wounded that he stays away from Johnson for a week, until they meet by chance. When Boswell confronts him with his rude behavior and painfully adds that no man has a greater respect and affection for him, Johnson uneasily insists that Boswell must have interrupted him. Boswell denies this, then continues to plead his case:

"But why treat me so before people who neither love you nor me?" JOHNSON. "Well, I am sorry for it. I'll make it up to you twenty different ways, as you please." BOSWELL. "I said to-day to Sir Joshua, when he observed that you *tossed* me sometimes—I don't care how often, or how high he tosses me, when only friends are present,—for then I fall upon soft ground: but I do not like falling on stones, which is the case when enemies are present.—I think this a pretty good image, Sir." JOHNSON. "Sir, it is one of the happiest I have ever heard." [8 May 1778]

Resolving their differences in a common admiration for Boswell's metaphor is perhaps an oblique way of dealing with the problem, but it is the way friendships work, and it generates a feeling of reconciliation and increased intimacy. As before, Boswell concludes with a generalizing statement: "The truth is, there was no venom in the wounds which he inflicted at any time, unless they were irritated by some malignant infusion by other hands" (8 May 1778). Their brief rift has become another brushstroke in Boswell's portrait of Johnson.

In the course of their friendship, both men grow in understanding. Johnson became an increasingly expert observer of Boswell's mercurial temperament and half-realized potentialities. An insight of his provides the *Life* with one of its early narrative climaxes. While the two men are at supper the night before Boswell is to leave for his study and travel on the continent, Johnson, seeing a moth flutter into the candle-flame, admonishes, "That creature was its own tormentor, and I believe its name was BOSWELL" (5 Aug. 1763). Johnson's knowledge of Boswell continued to grow. During their Hebridean tour, over ten years after their first meeting, Johnson reveals in a letter to Mrs. Thrale, appended to the third edition of the *Life* by Malone, that he has discovered new sides to Boswell:

Boswell will praise my resolution and perseverance, and I

shall in return celebrate his good humour and perpetual cheerfulness. He has better faculties than I had imagined; more justness of discernment, and more fecundity of images. It is very convenient to travel with him; for there is no house where he is not received with kindness and respect. [Note to Nov. 1773]

Despite the changes and minor setbacks in their friendship, Johnson sensed from the beginning Boswell's deep need for affection and approbation. Many of Johnson's assurances— all of them sincere expressions of his feelings—are found in letters written while they lived their separate lives in London and Edinburgh, and Boswell feared that Johnson was forgetting him. Like his prodding questions, Boswell's constant need of kind words sometimes annoyed Johnson: at one point, after once more expressing his affection, he tells Boswell to "write it down in the first leaf of your pocket-book and never doubt of it again" (23 Sept. 1777).[30]

Boswell's voracious appetite for Johnsoniana made his process of discovery endless. But since his incessant questioning molds Johnson in some ways, teasing potential parts of his personality and thought into actuality, the process is a complex one.[31] Without Boswell, is it likely that Johnson would ever have thought about what he would do if shut up in a

30. A similar sign of gentle irritation: "You always seem to call for tenderness. Know then, that in the first month of the present year I very highly esteem and very cordially love you. I hope to tell you this at the beginning of every year as long as we live; and why should we trouble ourselves to tell or hear it oftener?" (24 Jan. 1778).

Other examples in the *Life* of Johnson's assurance of his affection, many of them in his letters: 25 June 1763, 21 July 1763, 14 Jan. 1766, 15 March 1772, 24 Feb. 1773, 27 Aug. 1775, 23 Dec. 1775, 16 May 1776, 2 July 1776, 18 Feb. 1777, 11 Sept. 1777, 3 July 1778, 1 May 1779, 27 Oct. 1779, 14 March 1781, 21 March 1783.

31. See John Butt, *Biography in the Hands of Walton, Johnson and Boswell*, pp. 38–39.

castle with a newborn child? Not as clear-sighted as Johnson or as confident of his general conclusions, Boswell never tired of seeing Johnson in new contexts or of gathering new information about his past. There are, however, two places in the *Life* where he indicates a new perspective on Johnson, a clear giant step in his progress toward a greater understanding of the man. The first occasion is Boswell's return to London after his Grand Tour. He observes that seeing *"multorum hominum mores et urbes,"* has increased his veneration for Johnson. But, he adds:

> The roughness, indeed, which sometimes appeared in his manners, was more striking to me now, and from my having been accustomed to the studied smooth complying habits of the Continent; and I clearly recognized in him, not without respect for his honest conscientious zeal, the same indignant and satirical mode of treating every attempt to unhinge or weaken good principles. [15 Feb. 1766]

This observation is a significant stage in Boswell's ongoing attempt to discern general principles, or a meaningful pattern, in Johnson's behavior. The other passage, already quoted, concerns Boswell's realization one evening that he no longer sees the old aura of mystery about Johnson nor treats him with the usual "aweful reverence" (20 March 1778). Though he never ceased paying tribute to the marvelous complexity of Johnson's character, Boswell's growing awareness of Johnson as a friend, even a peer sometimes, adds a dimension of personal sympathy in the *Life* to what could have been merely a cold reverence for the Johnsonian achievement.

It is not necessary to catalogue all the vicissitudes of the friendship to see its general significance for the development of the *Life*. Without Johnson, Boswell would still have written a journal, though it is debatable whether he would have kept it so diligently. Nevertheless, in the Journal as it stands, Johnson is a major character second only to Boswell himself. So interwoven were the two life stories that Boswell seems never to have considered writing a fully objective biography; indeed, given his peculiar talent for first person narrative and dialogue, it is fortunate that he never attempted such a laborious task. But there is a deeper reason for Boswell's reluctance to exclude himself from the story of Johnson's life. Just as he tended to confuse art with life in other matters, so he considered his life and Johnson's as intricately wedded in actuality as they were in his Journal. When Boswell complains of their being apart for too long an interval, Johnson replies, "Then, Sir, let us live double" (end of 8 May 1781). More than Johnson could ever know, Boswell took this to heart. In mingling the stories of their lives, Boswell sometimes writes as though they have one life between them, as though the meaning of each life would be impoverished without the presence of the other.

A subtle example of this supposition at work is Boswell's use of Johnson's *Prayers and Meditations*. Although forty-two pages of the edition Boswell used included material written before 1763, he does not extensively use the collection to document Johnson's spiritual torment until after 1763.[32] The reason for this is that Boswell does not seriously try to depict Johnson's personal turmoil until they have met in 1763 and Boswell can know about these problems firsthand. After this point, he uses the *Prayers and Meditations* to reinforce his own observations. A more obvious manifestation of this double-life view is Boswell's excuse for including Johnson's letter praising his Journal as superior to the *Account of Corsica*. Boswell's explanation, which he puts in a footnote, is an excerpt from the *Account* on his desire to be known to

32. See *Prayers and Meditations, composed by Samuel Johnson, LL.D.,* collected by Rev. George Strahan, and note 19 in chapter one.

the world as an author: a good book captures the admirable parts of an author and immortalizes him, to be forever admired by distant peoples and generations (note to autumn 1769). The desire for immortality through universal admiration is Boswell's motive for publishing the *Account of Corsica,* the *Tour,* and the *Life;* this goal supplements rather than vitiates his didactic aim in portraying Johnson.

These two goals interact with Boswell's double aim of rendering the minute particulars of Johnson's life while indicating its overall significance and meaning. The two main topics of the *Life,* Johnson and his friendship with Boswell, are developed by subjecting the reader to a series of changes in narrative time and space, that is, in point of view. These changes in the *Life* involve thousands of movements toward or away from the historical moment. In painting his composite portrait of Johnson, Boswell was forced into many of these oscillations because of the nature of his materials; nevertheless, he managed to make a virtue of necessity by controlling this movement to achieve dramatic effects, a lively narrative, a deeper character portrayal, and a wider perspective of Johnson's significance.

Boswell's treatment of his friendship with Johnson involves a similar movement between immediacy and distance. By means of the brilliantly recorded conversations, Boswell enables us to join him with Johnson in his chambers, at the Club, at Reynolds's, at the Thrales', or sailing along the Thames. Sometimes Boswell is actually the topic of the conversation, not just its recorder, contributor, or catalyst. His search for universal meaning in a man's life leads him away from the immediacy of the historical moment just as it does in his Journal when he feels the need to take stock of himself. Boswell includes many of Johnson's compliments to him, assurances of affection, and reconciliations with him only to draw back as a biographer and cite them as examples of the great man's benevolence and candor. These incidents also aid Boswell in his own lifelong process of self-definition. In effect, he is often saying, "Since this episode involves Johnson's reactions to me, it is a brushstroke in my portrait as well as his." Because these details are examples or manifestations of a more generalized self in each of the men, some of the essential Johnsoniana is inseparable from the Boswelliana. Except for a few decorous omissions, the portrait of Johnson must be painted completely even if it entails revealing Boswell in an unfavorable light. To this end Boswell even includes his wife's cruel quip about the two of them: "I have seen many a bear led by a man: but I never before saw a man led by a bear" (note to 27 Nov. 1773). Although he adds that his wife's remark has "more point than justice," he repeats it as an example of the world's view of their friendship. Such an implicit general significance is Boswell's reason for including that drawn-out little history of the antagonism between his wife and Johnson, starting with his "irregular hours and uncouth habits" at her house, continuing with his very frequent yet lightly phrased pleas for her forgiveness in his letters, and culminating with her gift of a jar of orange marmalade to him, which he regards "as a token of friendship, as a proof of reconciliation, things much sweeter than sweetmeats" (22 July 1777).

The tension between authorial immediacy and distance in the *Life* ends with Boswell's formal good-bye to his readers in the section for November 1784. For the last few pages, Boswell eliminates himself from the narrative so that we can concentrate on the dying man as a suffering, lonely hero. By this time, Johnson has ceased radiating outward, warming the audience around him with revivifying rays; he is now a quiet center toward which is directed the attention of his sad friends and the sympathetic readers of the *Life*.

CHAPTER FOUR   *Boswell's Style:*
Like Curious Pieces of
Unmatched Porcelain

Boswell's attempt to give his
audience not only the flavor of Johnson's everyday experience but also an overview of the man produces oscillations,
contrasts, and temporal restlessness in the style as well as in
the structure and form of the *Life*. In his general comments
on style, Boswell seldom rises above cliché and the conventional wisdom of his time.[1] Much more enlightening are his
remarks on a specific style, especially his own or Johnson's.
While studying law in Holland, Boswell included in his self-
improvement program one or two pages of French theme-
writing every day. Since these French themes tend to be
direct translations of his English style, his criticisms of them

1. For instance: "Style is to sentiment what dress is to the person. The
effects of both are very great, and both are acquired and improved by
habit. When once we are used to it, it is as easy to dress neatly as like a
sloven; in the same way, custom makes us write in a correct style as easily
as in a careless inaccurate one" (*London Journal, 1762–1763*, p. 186). The
London Journal will be cited hereafter as *LJ*.

are significant.[2] He addresses his imaginary interlocutor in one of these themes:

> I have no intention of making you believe that I think by rule, that my sentences are so exact that they resemble a circle, which you have no difficulty in completing if you have made a segment of it. No, on the contrary, my sentences have no regular shape. My arguments, if you will, are sometimes circular, but my sentences are very much out of the ordinary. They are like curious porcelain, which the lady of the house has extreme difficulty in matching, so as to keep her set complete, when by ill luck a cup is broken. The same difficulty in finding a match is observable among excellent things; and, truly, I have reason at least to doubt whether my sentences are not very fine rather than very odd. Oddity itself is sometimes a kind of excellence.[3]

The oddity that Boswell sees in his writing is not a grand accumulation of willful idiosyncrasies, and not the verbal and syntactic picturesqueness of Burton, Browne, and Carlyle; it is rather an unpredictability that always threatens to catch the reader off balance, that never allows him to form confident expectations concerning the next phrase, clause, or sentence.

James Sutherland has noted that the prose of the early eighteenth century—of Addison, Steele, Swift, Pope, Fielding —achieves a balance between "the foreseen and the fortuitous."[4] Once a syntactic pattern has begun, only small changes are possible, and midstream reversals of grammar or

2. Pottle observes: "Though he became fluent in French, he never became really idiomatic or even accurate in that language; and if one substitutes the literal English equivalents, the result is usually good Boswellian English" (*Boswell in Holland, 1763–1764*, p. xix).

3. Ibid., pp. 79–80.

4. James Sutherland, "Some Aspects of Eighteenth-Century Prose," p. 99.

emphasis are evidence that the writer simply has not thought out what he wants to say. But literary periods overlap. While Addison's style was still a model for schoolboys, this balance between the foreseen and the fortuitous in prose was tottering, and schoolmasters, as well as men of letters, were opting for one side or the other. Hugh Blair's *Lectures on Rhetoric and Belles Lettres* (1783), together with other earlier books on style, criticized Addison's style as too loose, and offered renovated *Spectator* passages in which the conversational disorder had been written out.[5] To varying degrees there is also a stiffening in the prose of Johnson, Gibbon, Goldsmith, and Reynolds. Johnson's rigid, authoritative, and sometimes predictable prose is the example par excellence of a style in which the fortuitous has been reduced to a minimum.[6] On the other hand, at the same time there arose the incredible phenomenon of *Tristram Shandy* (1759–67), with its host of imitators straining to catch the wacky balance of progression and digression in Sterne, who prided himself on not being able to say things straight or even to finish a sentence.

Although both trends in prose style can be seen in the second half of the eighteenth century, the movement away from conversational looseness was definitely stronger in England during Boswell's adult years. He seems to have been caught in the middle, however, for his "invincible mediocrity" predisposed him to write in an uneccentric style and to see life

5. Ian A. Gordon, *The Movement of English Prose*. See Hugh Blair, *Lectures in Rhetoric and Belles Lettres,* ed. Harold F. Harding, *lecture 7.*

6. "In Johnson's prose the foreseen triumphs continually over the fortuitous; nothing is set down that is not the outcome of calm and mature deliberation. . . . The attraction of Johnson's prose lies to a large extent in the complete confidence which it induces; whether he launches himself upon a long or short period one knows that his point will be made exactly as he means to make it, the emphasis always falling upon the right places, and the rhythm coming to a regular close with the completion of the thought" (Sutherland, "Eighteenth-Century Prose," p. 103).

in terms of the average man's responses.[7] This is not to say that most people share Boswell's neurotic personality (though many would admit it if they shared his candor, too). Whatever his situation, no matter how heady or bizarre, he almost always attempts to show its connection with common behavior rather than to seek what is unique in the experience. Boswell was extremely aware of literary fashions, however, and his style reveals a tug-of-war between looseness and formality, moving as it does back and forth between Johnson's authority and Sterne's incorrigible formlessness.[8] The dynamics of this movement will become clear after a closer look at the *Life.* But since Boswell's prose undergoes no great change after the *London Journal,* we will first briefly examine this work, and then the *Hypochondriack* essays, to see better the stylistic polarities of looseness and rigidity which are more skillfully balanced in the *Life,* and therefore not so exaggerated and discernible.

The oscillation between immediacy and formality in Boswell's style exists in the *London Journal* of 1762–63 as well as in the *Hypochondriack* essays, which were finished only a few years before he began writing the *Life.* The emphases, of course, are different, since the first is an informal personal record (though it is written with a good deal of artistic awareness) and the second is a published series of essays (though they attempt to be chatty).

Despite his general interest in linguistics and his friendships with the grammarians Lowth and Johnson, the rhetoricians Blair, Kames, and George Campbell, and the elocu-

7. The phrase is Pottle's, from *James Boswell: The Earlier Years, 1740–1769,* p. 89. See also Pottle's "Boswell Revalued," pp. 79–91.

8. In the 1760s Boswell's dabbling in the Shandean manner produced "Observations on Squire Foote's The Minor," "The Cub at Newmarket: A Tale," and the posthumously published "Poetical Epistle to Tristram Shandy." See *Earlier Years,* pp. 50, 61, 62–64, 71–72.

tionist Thomas Sheridan, Boswell strove in the *London Journal* for a personal manner of turning his periods and varying his phrasing rather than emulating the accepted models of grammatic and stylistic correctness.[9] Since he intended that the *London Journal* be read only by Johnston and a few other friends, he could afford to make few concessions to public rules. He did not have to scrub up his informal style as he did in his letters to Erskine before they were brashly thrust upon the public in the *Letters between the Hon. Andrew Erskine and James Boswell Esq.* (1763). Indeed, even the artistic self-consciousness of the *London Journal* diminishes with the later Journals, which become increasingly private.[10] Most noticeable in this early journal is the great amount of conversation and the loose style which Boswell uses even when he is addressing himself.

Boswell writes many clusters of short, choppy sentences that serve as summary, the elaboration of a point, or the narration of rapid action. As he revised his Journals for the *Life,* he usually combined many of these shorter sentences in deference to popular notions of sentence length and rhythm. For this reason, the Journals often sound more "modern" than the corresponding passages in the *Life.* In the *London Journal,* summary and elaboration in brief sentences are his response to Lady Northumberland's kind offer to receive him whenever he calls:

> This put me into the finest humour. I thanked her sincerely. I chatted easily. She then carried me to my Lord, who was very glad to see me and very civil to me. This is indeed a noble family in every respect. They live in a most princely manner, perfectly suitable to their rank. Yet they

9. Esther K. Sheldon, "Boswell's English in the *London Journal,*" p. 1092.

10. Geoffrey Scott notes the increasing privateness of the Journals in "The Making of the *Life of Johnson,*" p. 66.

are easy and affable. They keep up the true figure of old English nobility. [*LJ*, p. 71]

Later, the same device conveys the extreme agitation of Boswell's mind:

This was one of the blackest days that I ever passed. I was most miserably melancholy. I thought I would get no commission, and thought that a grievous misfortune, and that I was very ill used in life. I ruminated of hiding myself from the world. I thought of going to Spain and living there as a silent morose Don. Or of retiring to the sweeter climes of France and Italy. But then I considered that I wanted money. I then thought of having obscure lodgings, and actually looked up and down the bottom of Holborn and towards Fleet Ditch for an out-of-the-way place. How very absurd are such conceits! Yet they are common. [*LJ*, pp. 213–14]

This passage serves also to exhibit two other traits of Boswell's journal style. The third and eighth sentences are typical of Boswell's fondness for main clauses linked simply by "and." His choppy sentences need only additive conjunctions to make them paratactic. The effect of alternating long and short sentences is also apparent here. Boswell often uses this alternation to vary the rhythm and syntax of his prose.[11] When he does subordinate his clauses, his favorite conjunctions are adversatives, especially "and yet"—a phrase particularly suitable for one who naturally uses the debate form, even when he is talking only to himself.

Many of these choppy passages may be loosely considered as rhythmic units. In both of the above examples, there is a

11. See for instance the long passage in *LJ*, pp. 199–201: "This afternoon I was very high-spirited and full of ambition. . . . I thought I might go to the Church-of-England Chapel, like Pitfour; and, in short, might live in the most agreeable manner."

longer sentence near the middle which slows the tempo of
the passage somewhat, and then the short sentences continue
until the final one, which, taking a relatively broad perspective, carries more than its share of the total section's meaning, bringing the unit to a close. Not all of Boswell's choppy
passages follow this pattern, but enough of them do to make
it characteristic of his style. Another example of this technique is Boswell's coda to the Louisa affair:

> Thus ended my intrigue with the fair Louisa, which I
> flattered myself so much with, and from which I expected
> at least a winter's safe copulation. It is indeed very hard.
> I cannot say, like young fellows who get themselves clapped
> in a bawdy-house, that I will take better care again. For I
> really did take care. However, since I am fairly trapped, let
> me make the best of it. I have not got it from imprudence.
> It is merely the chance of war. [*LJ*, p. 161]

The passages that follow this general pattern are miniature
examples of Boswell's tendency to move, almost like a movie
camera, in upon a moment and then to draw back (here, very
slightly) for a larger comment on the specific action.

Boswell's use of initial connectives further contributes to
the conversational informality of the *London Journal*. He is
vague about the logical relationships between clauses, just
as most of us would be if our casual thoughts or words were
set down directly on paper. Boswell uses "and so" and "so
that" interchangeably, meaning "therefore" or "with the result that." "So that" almost always appears in its vaguer and
more colloquial sense in a result rather than a purpose
clause: "There was a very full meeting, and many people of
my acquaintance, so that I was at my ease and had plenty of
conversation" (*LJ*, p. 142). Moreover, he tends to use "as" for
"since" in everything he ever wrote; this practice is common
in Addison and Fielding, but it becomes confusing when

there are "as-so" comparisons that interfere with the causal meaning of "as" when it appears. This confusion arises chiefly in *The Hypochondriack,* where Boswell's expository passages contain both constructions. Another vagueness, which Blair castigates in his *Lectures,* is the use of "which" when it has no clear antecedent.

> Mrs. Gould has never had any children, but has a great affection for her husband's, which I admire much. [*LJ,* p. 66]

> I went to St. James's Park, and, like Sir John Brute, picked up a whore. For the first time did I engage in armour, which I found but a dull satisfaction. [*LJ,* p. 227]

Occasionally Boswell's spontaneity creates genuine problems of clarity. He may begin a sentence with a general observation using the third person singular and, without warning, conclude with pronouns and verbs in the first person singular.

> I was observing to my friend Erskine that a plan of this kind [for keeping a journal] was dangerous, as a man might in the openness of his heart say many things and discover many facts that might do him great harm if the journal should fall into the hands of my enemies. [*LJ,* p. 39]

> You cannot get a man to undergo the drudgery of the law who only want to pass his life agreeably, and who thinks that my Lord Chancellor's four and twenty hours are not a bit happier than mine. [*LJ,* p. 90][12]

12. In the *Life* there are much less serious, but equally confusing shifts: "My readers will, I trust, excuse me for being thus minutely circumstantial, when it is considered that the acquaintance of Dr. Johnson was to me a most valuable acquisition, and laid the foundation of whatever instruction and entertainment they may receive from my collection concerning the great subject of the work which they are now perusing" (24 May 1763).

These are the worst offenses in the *London Journal;* there are far more in *The Hypochondriack.* Confusion results from a lack of control in Boswell's tendencies to shift points of view and to attempt to strike a balance between the general and the particular. In the *Life,* Boswell does not allow these tendencies to interfere with the communication of his meaning. Another way in which Boswell shifts his point of view quickly is to use different tenses within one passage. This trait, obvious in the *London Journal,* can be seen throughout his other Journals and Journal-derived works. After little more than two weeks of keeping his London Journal, Boswell voices his impatience with unnecessarily fastidious notions of tense:

> I have all along been speaking in the perfect tense, as if I was writing the history of some distant period. I shall after this use the present often, as most proper. Indeed, I will not confine myself, but take whichever is most agreeable at the time. [*LJ*, p. 65]

If these stylistic traits help create the conversational informality of the *London Journal,* what is Boswell's high style, proper to moments of Olympian moralizing and noble emotions? It would be wrong to speak of a "tension" between the formal and the unbuttoned in the *London Journal,* which is a fairly private record, not intended for publication. Boswell was too immersed in its events to include long digressions on the eternal verities suggested by his experience. Some such passages were added later when he was revising for the *Life.* There are, however, places in the *London Journal* where we can see Boswell striving for a rhetorical effect. Sometimes he employs parallel series, as when he muses on whether he should become a lawyer:

> I wanted much to be a man of consequence, and I con-

sidered that I could only be that in my own country. . . . I
also considered that the law was my plain road to prefer-
ment. That if I would go to the Scotch bar I would soon
be well employed. . . . I considered that the law seemed to
be pointed out by fate for me. That the family of Auchinleck had been raised by it. That I would soon be made Advocate Depute. . . . I considered that my notions of an advocate were false. That I connected with that character low
breeding and Presbyterian stiffness, whereas many of them
were very genteel people. That I might have the wit and
humour of Sir David Dalrymple . . . [and so on for several
sentences] [*LJ*, p. 200][13]

This is an elaborate example of Boswell's use of parallel sentences. His series usually run for only four or five sentences,
and they may be varied somewhat, as in the above passage
where he contemplates fleeing to Spain, France, or Italy.

Other kinds of series that Boswell uses are the doublet and
triplet. The repeated element may be an adjective, noun,
phrase, or clause. To be sure, there is nothing idiosyncratic
about binary constructions in eighteenth-century prose; they
may be found in Gibbon, Goldsmith, Addison, Fielding, and
particularly Johnson. What does seem to be special in the
London Journal is Boswell's excessive use of triplets. A count
in the Yale edition reveals fifty-eight triplets in the first thirty-
six pages. These triplets are of two basic types. The first type
is simply narrative summary, in which the repeated elements
may be single or, for variation, compound. Although the elements are usually verbs, they may also be nouns that suggest
action.

I then breakfasted at Child's Coffee-house, read the political papers, and had some chat with citizens. [*LJ*, p. 51]

13. See also the parallel use of "you" in the passage "We then walked
into the City. . . . Here and there you see a solitary bencher sauntering
about" (*LJ*, p. 234).

We set off at six; breakfasted at Alnwick, where we had with us a Captain Elliot of the East Indies, and were hearty. [*LJ*, p. 43]

The noise, the crowd, the glare of shops and signs agreeably confused me. [*LJ*, p. 44]

This raised my spirits, gave me notions of my consequence, and filled me with grandeur. [*LJ*, p. 65]

Some time after I came to London, I met with Mr. Mayne from Scotland, who reminded me that he had got me admitted a member of the Society for the Encouragement of Arts and Sciences in the year 1760; that the subscription was two guineas a year, and that three years were now unpaid, so that I owed six guineas. [*LJ*, p. 60]

The other kind of triplet that Boswell uses frequently in the *London Journal* is descriptive and evaluative rather than narrative.

I found my companion a jolly honest plain fellow. [*LJ*, p. 42]

A kind-hearted, plain, sensible man. . . . [*LJ*, p. 44]
A member of that elegant, useful, and noble Society. . . . [*LJ*, p. 61]

A sensible learned man, a good philosopher, and an excellent physician. [*LJ*, p. 48]

His Majesty spoke better than any man I ever heard: with dignity, delicacy, and ease. [*LJ*, p. 49]

Lord Elibank is a man of strong genius, great reading, and lively imagination. [*LJ*, p. 56]

Many four-part constructions also occur in the first half of the *London Journal*, but these, with the triplets, become increasingly rare in the latter two-thirds of the work. In the

Life, Boswell's use of them is not excessive, or idiosyncratic. The reason for the change cannot, of course, be definitely stated. Insofar as Boswell was aware of this stylistic mannerism, he may have rejected it as stiff and formulaic. It is significant that he begins using the triplets less frequently when he starts including conversations, such as the dialogues at Child's. Perhaps his closer attention to dialogue made him more aware of the various resources of language, aware of other less rigid ways of achieving the same effects.

Boswell did, however, possess an expository style for dealing with general observations and communicating factual information. This style, of which we see only a glimmer in the bustling *London Journal,* occurs more often during his later career as a periodical hack, literary prankster, reporter, and tireless journal-keeper. The fullest example of Boswell's expository style, with its few strengths and many weaknesses, is the series of essays that appeared in the *London Magazine* from October 1777 to August 1783 as *The Hypochondriack.* There is no doubt that in writing these essays Boswell learned things that stood him in good stead for the *Life.* Although Margery Bailey, the editor of the essays, sees Boswell's development as an all-too-neat three-stage process—the self-conscious artist, the conscientious craftsman, and the philosopher—there are many indications of his increasing skill in handling the essay form.[14] Since he regarded the ability to illustrate a point as most important to a "philosophical" writer, it is not surprising that we find him becoming more adept in marshaling his examples: rarely in the later numbers does he inelegantly paraphrase his quotations,[15] become sidetracked by their irrelevant details,[16] or rigidly enumerate a list.[17]

14. *The Hypochondriack,* ed. Margery Bailey, 1: 70.
15. Ibid., 1: 139–40.
16. Ibid., 1: 166.
17. Ibid., 1: 209–10.

This skill in handling authorities and primary materials rescues the *Life* from being what it sometimes becomes in its worst passages, a mere catalogue of Johnsoniana. In the use of allusions, as in so many other matters, Boswell had to learn restraint. He learned to avoid a bottleneck of references and quotations, such as the one in the second number where five sentences (sentences 11–15) must make room for six examples.[18] By using allusions more sparingly, Boswell could introduce them more gracefully, as in the sixty-ninth number on diaries. Another device that Boswell uses with growing caution is the elaborately detailed comparison and contrast. Frequently his clumsiness is amusing; perceiving this, he included in a moment of self-irony as the tenth number a much earlier written gloriously awkward comparison of Truth to a pair of shoes. Too often, however, this watered-down Johnsonian parallelism gets out of hand, as in the fourth number, where the use of balanced pairs becomes an unconscious habit that produces unnecessarily strained writing.[19]

Thus we see Boswell in *The Hypochondriack* becoming better able to handle his materials, to strike a balance and proportion between his own writing and the interspersed primary matter. We shall be disappointed, however, if we expect to see a steady progression toward competence in the details of his verbal style. Given what we know of Boswell's unstable personality and conflicting allegiances, this lack of progress is understandable. His style in *The Hypochondriack,* as well as in the *Life,* can better be described in terms of vectors than fixed qualities.[20] The main vectors of Boswell's essay style may be loosely described, at one end, as formal, stilted, florid, and awkward; at the other, as fluid,

18. Ibid., 1: 112–14.

19. Pointed out by Bailey in ibid., 1: 67.

20. For a modest attempt at a vector-description of style, see John B. Carroll, "Vectors of Prose Style."

natural, conversational, and plain. Indeed, if we maintain that prose style is a characteristic pattern of choices in diction and syntax, then we might feel uneasy about calling Boswell's essay manner a style at all. No significant change appears from month to month in paragraph length, total number of sentences per issue, or certain stilted constructions, such as a noun clause beginning with "that" used as the subject of a sentence. An exception, generally indicative of his growing skill in the form, is his later use of slightly shorter sentences. His vacillation in sentence construction is mirrored in the rapid alternation of his tone between chattiness and pomposity.

Boswell intends that his *Hypochondriack* essays be chatty: "I do not impose upon myself the talk of regular system or exact order; but just throw out what thoughts occur to me, as if I were sitting with a friend."[21] The attempt to catch the graceful informality of urbane conversation in one's prose style goes at least as far back as the Restoration gentleman.[22] The stylistic device that does most to create a conversational looseness in Boswell's essays in his use of transitional words or connectives, at or near the beginning of a clause. These words, all used to establish a chatty sentence-to-sentence continuity, are of three kinds. First, Boswell may repeat the key words of an already stated plan, as in the opening of the first number where he mentions how happy an invention the English periodical is, "whether we consider the advantage of writers, or of readers." The second sentence begins, "To writers, it affords. . . ." and the seventh sentence, "To readers, a periodical paper affords. . . ." Boswell uses this rather heavy-handed device less frequently and more gracefully in later numbers. The second kind of transition is that which refers

21. *Hypochondriack*, 1: 84. See also 1: 314–15, 331; 2: 32, 54.

22. See the sketch of Restoration prose in James Sutherland's *On English Prose*, pp. 79–80.

to, but does not repeat, the key words of the argument. These words are "such," "this," and "that," and may be adjective or substantive. The third type of connective refers to the logical steps in the argument. These words, by far the most numerous of the three types, include "indeed," "too," "therefore," "for," "but," "even," "then," "however," "yet," and "accordingly." The most common of these is "but," which sometimes begins two or three consecutive sentences.[23]

Boswell's loose sentence constructions also contribute to the chatty tone of the essays. With only moderate success, he leaves dependent clauses standing as independent sentences.[24] In general, Boswell's use of short sentences in the essays is effective; this habit, however, is the positive side of his overall tendency to indulge his love of variety until he is sidetracked and forced to say things like "But I intended to say. . . ." and "But I should get back to. . . ." In long sentences, he often scrambles the natural subject-verb-object order or interrupts it with parenthetical and digressive re-

23. *Hypochondriack* no. 70 has many transition words of all three kinds; the most common is "but," which begins sentences number 3, 13, 26, 29, 34, 42, 51, 52, 56. Louis T. Milic has noted Swift's extensive use of these initial connectives in "Unconscious Ordering in the Prose of Swift," pp. 87–90. He observes that Swift's favorite connectives are additive, adversative, and causal, the most frequent being "but." This is, he says, "merely a fraction of the available possibilities." Moreover, Swift most often uses these connectives not "notionally but syntaxically," that is, to serve some "vague rhetorical function" rather than to articulate a step in a truly logical argument. All of these remarks apply as well to Boswell's style in *The Hypochondriack;* the obvious differences in their styles stem from other matters, chiefly from Swift's passion for clarity in his diction and syntax. To use Frye's term again (cf. chap. 2, n. 21), the use of these connectives betrays the heavy influence of the colloquial associative rhythm on the prose of Swift and Boswell, that is, their frequent desire to deny or postpone the finality of each period as much as possible. Sustained through a variety of devices, this associative momentum exists in much of the *Life* as well as *The Hypochondriack.*

24. Even so admiring a critic as Margery Bailey betrays her exasperation: see *Hypochondriack,* 2: 142n, 203n.

marks. Sentences that are grammatically neater may have many possible intonations, each with its shade of meaning; Boswell, however, patterns his sentences after their intonation, drastically limiting the meanings that are open to the reader. This stylistic device grows out of Boswell's need to reflect in the wanderings of syntax and topic the various uncertainties and qualifications that occur to him in the process of thinking and writing. Such a technique always risks the confusion of these sentences from *The Hypochondriack*. At best, they make the reader do a double take:

> That lovers of wine have rarely been good members of society in the decent mediocrity of ordinary parts, is a juster remark. For men of superior talents have been able to rise high, notwithstanding the impediment of a vice which would have depressed feebler spirits.[25]

> Without meaning to affect, being altogether convinced by that writer, I confess I am more and more of opinion that the wisest maxims are very old ones; for, that mankind have, in ages very early with respect to ours, observed by their natural sagacity, what is solidly true, and of consequence, permanent.[26]

Conflicting with the looseness of Boswell's style are the many devices that are borrowed from public oratory and formal writing. In *The Hypochondriack* Boswell does not control these two manners as well as he does in the *Life*. Almost every essay is a demonstration of mutual interference between formal and conversational tones. This clash creates an ambiguity in Boswell's relation to his audience: is he really just a friend talking things over with us, or does he consider himself a moralist, with an edge on us in experience and wis-

25. Ibid., 1: 331.
26. Ibid., 2: 81.

dom? Seldom in these essays does Boswell firmly decide whether he wants to write as if he is placing himself at the birth of his ideas (at the historical moment), or much later, at his desk, self-consciously and distantly addressing his audience about matters that he has had time to cogitate.

Even the free wheeling sentences cited above reveal the stiltedness of Boswell's expository style. Two favorite devices are a noun clause beginning with "that" used as the subject of a sentence and a clause with an impersonal verb. These constructions are related, for if most of Boswell's clauses using impersonal verbs were straightened out, their subjects would be noun clauses beginning with "that." Indeed, many of Boswell's sentences in *The Hypochondriack* are difficult to label either "stilted" or "conversational"; they are recklessly constructed units whose building blocks are fragments of formal and rhetorical prose. A partial explanation of the formality in Boswell's writing is that in the second half of the eighteenth century, there occurred a shift from a familiar to a more artificial and rhetorical style. This shift has been attributed by at least one scholar to the influence of the Scottish writers, who employed relatively formal rather than colloquial constructions because they did not have a sure command of idiomatic English.[27] Of course, Boswell's origin made him especially susceptible to this general influence.

Like the "Inviolable Plan," the essays were primarily a phase in Boswell's extensive self-improvement program, an intermittently successful project to improve his spirits simply by writing the hypochondria out of himself. Since his audience and his relation to it were secondary considerations which he nexer fixed or defined for himself, his essays lack the focus of a man who has (at least) a literary identity and is writing on a general or specific occasion to an audience

27. Sutherland, *On English Prose,* pp. 79–80.

with whom he shares or rejects certain attitudes. The essays become now immediate, now distant, regardless of their topic. Both subject and style go their own way. This restlessness can also be seen in the organization of the essays. The first two numbers are a dramatic example: in the first there is an extremely schematic progression from point to point, and the divisions between major ideas coincide with paragraph divisions. The second number, on the other hand, exhibits an obvious lack of order, particularly in the disproportionate amount of material that is crammed into the second paragraph (see Appendix 3). Wimsatt describes Johnson's style as "a formal exaggeration—in places a caricature—of a certain pair of complementary drives, the drive to assimilate ideas, and the drive to distinguish them—to collect and to separate."[28] The gulf between the styles of Johnson and Boswell is clear: Johnson's favorite constructions are parallels and antitheses, while Boswell's are qualifiers—clauses beginning with "but," "although," and "however," and modifying phrases early in a sentence before the main statement has been completed. At his best and worst, Boswell has neither the desire nor the discipline to think out his subject and order his remarks according to the nature of his ideas. This is Johnson's achievement. Boswell ends the series of essays on a note of wistful disappointment:

> I am closing the scene of a species of literary existence, in which I own I have experienced sometimes anxiety, and sometimes self-complacency. . . . I perceive they are not so lively as I expected they would be. But they are more learned.[29]

In the *Life of Johnson*, unlike *The Hypochondriack*, there

28. W. K. Wimsatt, Jr., *The Prose Style of Samuel Johnson*, foreword to 1963 edition.
29. *Hypochondriack*, 2: 299, 302.

is one specific occasion for Boswell's writing: the death of
Johnson, whose excellency and unique character must be
passed on to those who can never know him. This great purpose gives the *Life* a focus sharper than the essays could ever
have had. As in the *Hypochondriack* essays, there is in the
Life a wavering of authorial identity and relationship to the
reader, but these changes now enrich the total subject because
they grow out of Boswell's actual responses to Johnson and
himself. In the essays, the changes weaken any coherence in
the figure of "Mr. Hypochondriack" and thus throw into
question the whole dramatic premise relating Boswell to his
readers. It is not so much a question of Boswell's altering his
style, as of his eventually hitting upon a subject congenial to
his style. In addition, since the *Life* provides him with so
many legitimate occasions for different levels of style, he can
work out the proper manner for a short passage knowing
that his love of variety will be appeased by the shifts to come
in a page or two. For these reasons, there are in the *Life* far
fewer and less serious examples of Boswell's points of view
working at cross-purposes so as to destroy the effect of a
passage.

The polarity already noted in Boswell's essay style exists
also in the *Life*, though in opposite proportions of looseness
and formality. In general, the range of styles can be corre-
lated with the range of time levels from the historical moment to the time of composition. The following sentences
serve to remind readers of the *Life* of this range, as it stretches
from distance to immediacy, from formality to conversational
looseness.

What I consider as the peculiar value of the following
work, is, the quantity that it contains of Johnson's conversation; which is universally acknowledged to have been emi-
nently instructive and entertaining; and of which the speci-

mens that I have given upon a former occasion, have been received with so much approbation, that I have good grounds for supposing that the world will not be indifferent to more ample communications of a similar nature. [Undated introduction]

In this year I have not discovered a single private letter written by him to any of his friends. It should seem, however, that he had at this period a floating intention of writing a history of the recent and wonderful successes of the British arms in all quarters of the globe; for among his resolutions or memorandums, September 18, there is, "Send for books for Hist. of War." How much is it to be regretted that this intention was not fulfilled. [Early 1760]

His uncommon kindness to his servants, and serious concern, not only for their comfort in the world, but their happiness in the next, was another unquestionable evidence of what all, who were intimately acquainted with him, knew to be true. [March–April 1783]

He said, that for general improvement, a man should read whatever his immediate inclination prompts him to; though, to be sure, if a man has a science to learn, he must regularly and resolutely advance. [12 April 1776]

Vastly enriching the stylistic variety within the *Life* are the numerous contributions and primary documents interpolated by Boswell. The progression of the above sentences toward a greater immediacy is completed by the recorded conversations, which capture the loose associativeness in the thoughts of men and the constant surprise in their verbal interactions. Grammar and logic become less rigid the closer Boswell moves in upon the historical moment. The great exception to this, however, is Johnson himself. His intense mental and verbal discipline stands out against the backdrop

of conviviality and impulse. Always aware of this contrast,
Boswell makes use of it repeatedly:

> We discussed the question whether drinking improved
> conversation and benevolence. Sir Joshua maintained it
> did. JOHNSON. "No, Sir: before dinner men meet with
> great inequality of understanding; and those who are con-
> scious of their inferiority, have the modesty not to talk. . . .
> [12 April 1776]

Boswell's emendations in the manuscript of the *Life* are
a good indication of his stylistic values. In general, the section before 1763 (the year of their meeting) shows more
changes, with passages added, crossed out, and transposed.
The left margin of Boswell's sheets is extra large up to 1740
and only slightly smaller until 1763 to allow for the many
additions and corrections. There are two explanations for
these heavy emendations in the early part of the *Life*. First,
Boswell was characteristically more industrious at the beginning of his project, more fastidious and capable of more sustained exertions of editorial energy. Second, he appears to
be most confident in writing dialogue, little of which appears
before 1763. The change that Boswell most often makes in
dialogue is to strike out a small portion for the sake of relevance or decorum. Boswell's recorded conversations in his
Journal range from the short and cryptic to the elliptical to
the fully written. Where necessary, he expanded these passages for their inclusion in the *Life,* but he did not revise
them much in the manuscript. On the other hand, Boswell
corrects the passages in which he is relatively distant from the
historical moment, that is, when he is judging, evaluating,
describing in generalized terms, or writing reconstructed narrative. A dramatic example of this tendency occurs in manuscript pages 965–68 (15–24 June 1784). This section is framed
by two matters calling for Boswell's authorial intervention:

at the beginning he relates and evaluates Johnson's advice to young lawyers, and at the end, he carefully describes the efforts of Johnson's friends to secure an addition to his income in his last years. The latter was a touchy subject since there was a rumor, which Boswell wanted to lay to rest permanently, that Johnson had asked for this extra money. In between these two heavily emended passages Boswell's narrative and recorded conversations are strikingly clean. His emendations of conversational passages here and elsewhere are most often very small: one-word substitutions such as "there" for "here" or "were" for "was" or the deletion of one of the two synonyms he had written together when, earlier, he could not choose one over the other. Boswell's amplifications of a phrase, as well as his condensations of one, usually reveal a desire to be as faithful as possible to his meaning, to the implied or overt immediacy of an act.[30] Thus, the manuscript of the *Life* reveals where in the stylistic spectrum Boswell worked most comfortably, and how he had to labor to satisfy himself with passages involving relatively strict syntax and more elevated diction.

Even though the *Life* amply demonstrates Boswell's fondness for periodic sentences, his high rhetoric only occasionally leads him toward the pedantic stiltedness and incoherence common in *The Hypochondriack*. The style of the *Life* impresses most readers of eighteenth-century prose as simple, effective, and fluid. This impression is borne out by a glance at Boswell's many manuscript changes in the direction of simplicity. Also, responsible for the relatively unadorned style of the *Life* is its origin in the personal papers of Boswell

30. Examples of such small amplifications are "partly from a conscientious motive, being persuaded" for "partly from a conscientious persuasion" (MS, p. 177v) and "no interest in deceiving us" for "no interest to deceive" (MS, p. 263). The manuscript of the *Life* is in the collection of Boswell Papers at Yale University.

and other men.[31] Like the sentences in *The Hypochondriack,* those in the *Life* tend to consist of two parts which are either opposed to each other ("but," "yet") or loosely additive ("and," "and so," the vague "which"). Sometimes the adversative conjunction is replaced by a semicolon: "I said it was not fair to attack us thus unexpectedly; he should have warned us of our danger." In the *Life* he uses rather mechanically a set of transitional phrases to enable him, once he has mentioned the date and place of a meeting with Johnson, to get into the main topic as quickly as possible. These phrases are notable for the abruptness of their transitions: "Talking of ——, he said . . ."; "We talked of ——"; "—— being mentioned, so-and-so mentioned that . . ."; and other variations.

Boswell's desire for a formal grammatic order as well as for an ungrammatic looseness polarizes his style into two manners, each of which threatens to fall into an unreadable, incoherent excess. Although the *Life* tends toward looseness, it of course exhibits much greater control than his Journals. The simplicity of the *Life,* its apparent lack of artifice, and the transparency of its narrative style are the results of Bos-

31. Although he perhaps overstates the lack of rhetoric in the *Life,* Geoffrey Scott testifies to the work's simplicity: "It no doubt contributed to the strength of the final result that the first full record should have been of this private and unstudied character. Had Boswell composed in the first instance with an audience directly in view, he might probably have not avoided occasional lapses into the declamatory style which so often inflates his letters, published articles and pamphlets. He might have puffed his subject. One cannot tell; perhaps his sense of reverent discipleship towards Johnson might, even so, have sufficiently protected him. But it is certain that in its simplicity and absence of rhetoric the *Life of Johnson* resembles the private unliterary Journals rather than the other published works. . . . And if anything can increase our sense of the ascetic veracity of the *Life of Johnson* it is to read the narrative, as most of it was first written, mingled with the patient tale of Boswell's acts and hopes and humiliations, set down for his own solitary view" ("Making of the *Life,*" p. 67).

well's abiding faith in the value of each particular moment
he spent with Johnson and of each detail that he could re-
trieve from the past.

In the *Life* and his other works Boswell reveals a desire for
neatness and order. We see it in the periodic order of some
sentences, the logical sequence of points in his arguments,
and the antichronological arrangement of examples to prove
a claim. As in his own life, however, this search for order is
usually thwarted. Boswell's periodic sentences are sometimes
grotesque caricatures, the progression of his arguments as
indicated by his transition words is usually pseudological,
and the points made by his legalistic amassing of examples
are often clouded by the contradictory evidence that he faith-
fully records. In this way, Boswell avoids the oversimplifica-
tion of Walton's portrait of Donne. Two things work against
the achievement of a stable, orderly style in the *Life:* Boswell
treated his records as "portable soup," capable of almost
infinite dilution, and he commonly used conversation as the
model for his narrative style.

Boswell's compositional methods characteristically involved adding to his collection of Johnsoniana rather than
selecting and deleting material. At times the workings of his
memory resembled total recall as he fleshed out a skeleton of
rough notes or memoranda.[32] Clearly, this additive process
was incompatible with any kind of schematic master plan. A
similar additive process was at work as Boswell constructed
his sentences. Early in his journalizing (7 September 1761–
19 July 1762), Boswell experimented with Shelton's tachy-
graphy, the shorthand method used by Pepys.[33] Later, Boswell worked out his own system of shorthand, a system of

32. Frederick A. Pottle, "The Power of Memory in Boswell and Scott,"
pp. 174–75.
33. See Frederick A. Pottle, "Boswell's Shorthand," p. 545.

condensation that would allow him to expand at his leisure and yet be faithful to the original utterance. Good examples of this technique may be found by comparing Boswell's London Journal of 1778 with the corresponding sections of the *Life*. During the spring of this year, Boswell enjoyed a giddy round of breakfasts, dinners, and evening conversations. He records a great amount of dialogue, much of it with dramatic tags; there is hardly any introspection. The following passage is from an account of a lively dinner at Reynolds's on 9 April. Present with Boswell and the host were Bennet Langton, Lady Rothes, Richard Owen Cambridge, Allan Ramsay (the painter), Gibbon, the Bishop of St. Asaph, and Johnson.

> A. RAMSAY. "Literature upon the grow, in its spring in france. Here passed." JOHNS. "Literature was in France long before we had it. Paris second City for revival of letters. Italy first, to be sure. What have we done for literature like the Stephani, &c? Our literature we had through France. Caxton printed only two books, Chaucer & Gower y^t were not translations from the french, & Chaucer much from ye Italians. No, Sir, if Literature in its spring in France, 'tis a second spring, 'tis after a winter. We are before the french. But We hold Sun long after them. In england a Man who wears a sword & a powdered wig is ashamed to be illiterate. I believe 'tis not so in France.[34]

In the *Life* this passage underwent the following changes:

> RAMSAY. "Literature is upon the growth, it is in its spring in France. Here it is rather passée." JOHNSON. "Literature was in France long before we had it. Paris was the second city for the revival of letters: Italy had it first, to be sure. What have we done for literature, equal to what was done

34. Inge Probstein, "Boswell's London Journal of 1778," p. 42. Also *Boswell in Extremes, 1776–1778*, eds. Charles McC. Weis and Frederick A. Pottle, pp. 254–55.

by the Stephani and others in France? Our literature came
to us through France. Caxton printed only two books,
Chaucer and Gower, that were not translations from the
French; and Chaucer, we know, took much from the
Italians. No, Sir, if literature be in its spring in France, it
is a second spring; it is after a winter. We are now before
the French in literature; but we had it long after them. In
England, any man who wears a sword and a powdered wig
is ashamed to be illiterate. I believe it is not so in France.
[9 April 1778]

The expansions are slight here because Boswell is working
with an animated dialogue. This additive process is far more
elaborate in passages of narrative or authorial commentary.
His tendency to attach a clause or phrase loosely to his main
statement sometimes gets out of hand; the result is breath-
less, tongue-twisting sentences that try to say everything at
once. Boswell left such sentences unsimplified probably because he was too proud of himself for fitting in all of his information to notice that the end product bordered on the
unreadable.

That his love for his wife was of the most ardent kind, and,
during the long period of fifty years, was unimpaired by
the lapse of time, is evident from various passages in the
series of his *Prayers and Meditations,* published by the
Reverend Mr. Strahan, as well as from other memorials,
two of which I select, as strongly marking the tenderness
and sensibility of his mind. [17 March 1752]

I mentioned an acquaintance of mine, a sectary, who was
a very religious man, who not only attended regularly on
publick worship with those of his communion, but made a
particular study of the Scriptures, and even wrote a commentary on some parts of them, yet was known to be very

licentious in indulging himself with women; maintaining
that men are to be saved by faith alone, and that the Chris-
tian religion had not prescribed any fixed rule for the intercourse between the sexes. [26 March 1776]

The Life of POPE was written by Johnson *con amore,* both
from the early possession which that writer had taken of
his mind, and from the pleasure which he must have felt,
in for ever silencing all attempts to lessen his poetical fame
by demonstrating his excellence, and pronouncing the following triumphant eulogium:—"After all this, it is surely
superfluous to answer the question that has once been
asked, Whether Pope was a Poet? otherwise than by asking
in return, If Pope be not a poet, where is poetry to be
found?" [Early 1781]

These sentences are precisely the sort censured by Adam
Smith's lectures on rhetoric at Glasgow University, which
Boswell attended, and by Hugh Blair's very similar *Lectures
on Rhetoric and Belles Lettres* (1783), which Boswell heard
Blair, later his literary mentor, deliver at the University of
Edinburgh in 1760–61.[35] In his *Lectures,* Blair agrees with

35. Boswell's experience with Smith's lectures has been summarized by
Pottle in "Boswell's University Education," p. 248: "Smith began with
some general remarks on language, went on to consider the proper construction of sentences and the different kinds of style proper for different
subjects, and then analysed at considerable length the styles of various
great historians and orators, mainly of Greece and Rome. This would all
have been of great interest to a youthful author of Boswell's stamp and
education, but even more exciting would have been Smith's constant
concrete references to a large number of English authors, some of them
living: Addison, Bolingbroke, Burnet, Clarendon, Congreve, Dryden,
Gray, Hervey, Hobbes, Lee, Macpherson, Mandeville, Milton, Otway,
Pope, Shaftesbury, Shakespeare, Shenstone, Spenser, Swift, Temple,
Thomson, Waller, and Young. Smith dismissed the traditional pedantries
of rhetorical taxonomy with open contempt, and addressed himself
throughout to the task of teaching a direct, clean, but not necessarily
'simple' style. He distinguished between the 'plain' style, of which
Swift was his great exemplar, and the 'simple,' which he illustrated by

the other schoolmen of his time in condemning conversation
as a model for prose style. In lectures 10–13 he warns against
mixing the periodic style with the style coupé, switching
points of view within a sentence, using the loose connectives
"and" or "and so" rather than making logical relationships
explicit, and crowding too much into one sentence. Boswell
does all of these in the *Life,* largely because of the conversational looseness that he prized in his expository and narrative styles. Blair, however, is confusing on this matter: he
frequently emphasizes the importance of variety in one's
writing, even to the point of looseness and harshness, yet he
relies heavily on the maxim that a good style is a clear style.
He never works out a clear case for stylistic variety or clarity.
More importantly, he does not demonstrate how to accom-
modate these two values to one's personal style. Thus the
Lectures may have reinforced the conversational tone of
Boswell's style, even though Blair specifically inveighs against
this manner of writing. At any rate, Blair's *Lectures* reveal
the age's ambivalence concerning matters of style.

Blair also talks about the many kinds of simplicity in style,
one of which exactly describes "the typically Boswellian
manner" of the Journals, the *Tour,* and the *Life.* This type
of simplicity is based on "the easy and natural manner in
which our Language expresses our thoughts" and "is compatible with the highest ornament." The main characteristic
is that the writer "expresses himself in such a manner, that
every one thinks he could have written in the same way."[36]

Sir William Temple. Both 'plain' and 'simple' styles he considered
good. His exemplars of bad style were Shaftesbury and, apparently in the
lectures that Boswell heard, Johnson."

Boswell's early friendship with Blair is recounted in the *LJ.,* pp. 234,
236, 253–54, 258, 259.

36. Blair, *Lectures,* 1: 389–90.

The highest degree of this Simplicity, is expressed by a French term, to which we have none that fully answers in our Language, *naïveté*. . . . That sort of amiable ingenuity, or disguised openness, which seems to give us some degree of superiority over the person who shows it; a certain infantine Simplicity, which we love in our hearts, but which displays some features of the character that we think we could have art enough to hide; and which, therefore, always leads us to smile at the person who discovers this character.[37]

From his long experience of journal-keeping and his friends' reactions to his writing, Boswell knew that simplicity was the great strength of his records, and that he could pursue it in the whole range of his styles, from plain to formal. Moreover, Blair probably appeared to him to approve the conversational style in some way, because it seemed (at least to Boswell) to be the proper vehicle for this kind of simplicity.

The ambiguity in Blair's *Lectures* derives from his inability, as a sympathetic reader, to deny the appeal of various styles. His description of the increasing refinement of English prose is much like Hurd's and Thomas Warton's wistful assessments of what the neoclassic age had lost by writing Spenser out of its accepted poetic canon.[38] Blair's history of English prose style begins with "some of our earliest classics in the English language," that is, Raleigh, Bacon, Hooker, Chillingworth, Milton, Harrington, Cudworth, and others in the reigns of Elizabeth, James I, and Charles I. These men wrote in the "Nervous Style," which today, says Blair, sounds

37. Ibid., p. 391.
38. Richard Hurd, *Letters on Chivalry and Romance*, and Thomas Warton, *Observations on the Faerie Queene of Spenser*. René Wellek discusses the problems that these critics had accommodating Spenser to the tenets of neoclassical criticism in *The Rise of English Literary History*, pp. 103–04, 166–70.

harsh because of its violent inversions, unusual diction, and general neglect of "smoothness and ease." Blair attributes the harshness of the "Nervous Style" to the fact that it "was indeed entirely formed upon the idiom and construction of the Latin in the arrangement of Sentences." Blair, however, finishes his paragraph by giving this older style its due:

> Yet some advantages certainly attended this sort of Style; and whether we have gained, or lost, upon the whole, by departing from it, may bear a question. By the freedom of arrangement, which it permitted, it rendered the Language susceptible of more strength, of more variety of collocation, and more harmony of period. But however this be, such a style is now obsolete; and no modern writer could adopt it without the censure of harshness and affectation. The present form which the Language has assumed, has, in some measure, sacrificed the study of strength to that of perspicuity and ease. Our arrangement of words has become less forcible, perhaps, but more plain and natural: and this is now understood to be the genius of our Language.[39]

Dryden, Blair continues, was most responsible for the stylistic shift toward "perspicuity and ease"; but since even he had his faults, writers after him have concerned themselves with "Purity and Elegance of Style." Blair concludes that this movement appears to be progress, a steady realization of the "genius" of the English language, but that, nevertheless, "we are far from the strength of several of the Greek and Roman authors."[40]

As a guide for the would-be stylist, Blair ultimately fails because he is too honest to give unequivocal praise to the style that he is trying to teach through his numerous revisions of such modern writers as Addison. Since the new elegance was

39. Blair, *Lectures*, 1: 378.
40. Ibid., 1: 379.

a bittersweet victory in Blair's eyes, Boswell could feel, on some level, that he had been given permission to subvert it by either the relatively slapdash virtuosity of Dryden or the stately rhetoric of Hooker. For Boswell, already committed to the informal manner of the Journals for which Johnson and other friends praised him highly, the refinements of Dryden and Addison would be unbearable restrictions. In addition, Boswell had the highest praise for Johnson's prose, another negative example used by Smith and Blair.

Despite his interest in linguistic matters and his friendships with a number of professors, Boswell persevered in the use of conversation as a model for his style. Even some of his stilted sentences retain, as we have seen, a certain conversational looseness. Although writing sentences with conversational syntax and rhythm ran counter to most of the popular books on style, a high regard for the social value of conversation was very much in keeping with conventional wisdom. During the Restoration, the conversation of gentleman was thought to be the proper model for all prose writing. Even after this had gone out of literary fashion after the turn of the century, the process of genteel conversation was still regarded as one of man's most powerful instruments for discovering the truth. This attitude is part of the strong sense of society in neo-classic England: it is largely responsible for the popularity of Horatian rather than Juvenalian satire, and is connected with the numerous clubs and salons which have ever since been popular with clubbable Englishmen, but which, by Johnson's death, were becoming increasingly dissociated from the earnest and productive literary life of the country. Boswell reflects this view of conversation's social utility when he assures the readers of *The Hypochondriack* that his essays will have the informal disorder of a talk between friends. Fielding, whose style is relatively formal, is more explicit. He regards conversation as "the only accurate guide to knowledge":

The primitive and literal sense of this word, is, I appre-
hend, to turn round together; and in its more copious usage
we intend by it, that reciprocal interchange of ideas, by
which truth is examined; things are, in a manner, turned
round, and sifted, and all our knowledge communicated
to each other.[41]

Johnson reveals in his *Dictionary* the same broad interpretation of the word, still reflecting the force of its Latin origin:
"conversation. Commerce; intercourse; familiarity."

We have seen that the conversational aspects of Boswell's
style are the result of his sensitivity to dramatic effects, the
wayward rhythms and syntactic relationships that can emphasize the experiential nature of the most abstract idea. His
more elaborate periodic sentences also reveal this sensitivity,
but the effect is achieved by skillfully delaying the final key
words, whereas in his plainer style Boswell avoids all such
manipulation by following the unfolding of thoughts and
events as they occur. In this way, he is better able to focus
directly on the narrative event without dissipating its inherent drama either in distracting considerations for grammatic
orotundity, or in establishing an expansive point of view.
This fondness for conversational rhythms is part of his delight
in dialogue, which sometimes led him to cast even his own
Journals in the form of a debate. Occasionally Boswell's style
and skill in capturing dialogue, together with his use of
dramatic tags, make parts of the *Life* strongly resemble a

41. Henry Fielding, "An Essay on Conversation," in *Works*, ed. W. E.
Henley, 14: 246. See also Sterne in *Tristram Shandy*, ed. J. A. Work,
2.11.108–09: "Writing, when properly managed, (as you may be sure I
think mine is) is but a different name for conversation: As no one, who
knows what he is about in good company, would venture to talk all;
—so no author, who understands the just boundaries of decorum and
good breeding, would presume to think all: The truest respect which you
can pay to the reader's understanding, is to halve this matter amicably,
and leave him something to imagine, in his turn, as well as yourself."

comedy of manners in prose.[42] But it is only in limited sections of the *Life* that we can see Boswell imitating such models, and even his tendency to imitate the looseness of conversation yields to his full-blown periodic sentences or the formal tone of many of the letters. In the *Life* Boswell charts his course—a remarkably successful one—between these two styles, each with its potential for incoherent excess. This is a risky kind of writing, and his reasons for taking these risks lead ultimately to his attitudes toward language and experience.

42. See Sven Eric Molin, "Boswell's Account of the Johnson-Wilkes Meeting."

CHAPTER FIVE   *Boswell's Image*
of the Past

In the opening sentences of
the *Life* Boswell cannot help referring to the all-too-obvious
irony that he should be undertaking the biography of a man
who was generally acknowledged to be a master biographer.
He observes with regret that "had Dr. Johnson written his
own life . . . the world would probably have had the most
perfect example of biography that was ever exhibited." Un-
fortunately, he adds, Johnson's autobiographical writings
consisted only of numerous particulars which "he never had
persevering diligence enough" to arrange "into a regular
composition" and most of which were "consigned by him to
the flames, a few days before his death" (beginning of undated introduction). At this point, Boswell expresses the
hope that he, an unusually privileged observer of Johnson's
life, may do much to remedy this loss. Boswell's attitude toward his subject is elegiac, especially since rereading his
Journals before writing the *Life* recalled for him not only his
own lost opportunities but also the pervasive influence of
Johnson's melancholy. As in some other elegies, *Lycidas* and
Adonais for example, the occasion leads the writer to con-
template the value of his craft and to make this contempla-

tion part of his general subject. Although Boswell's tone in his Journals is not usually elegiac, he is still writing to reclaim the past, and it is this feeling of time passing, this straining to reconstitute the important parts of something possibly lost, that characterizes his obsession with his past and determines some of his basic attitudes in the *Life* toward language and experience.[1]

Because Boswell's literary style changed very little during his career, and because some of his writing smells of midnight oil, we are perhaps surprised to see him constantly fascinated by stylistic and linguistic matters; and yet, throughout his writings are sprinkled an enormous variety of observations on language. His profound wonder for the mystery of language is unmistakable: it grew with his early campaign to purge himself of Scotticisms; it continued with his project of learning French while in Utrecht and on his Grand Tour; it must have deepened during friendly exchanges with his mentors Kames and Blair; and it certainly increased during his long important apprenticeship for the *Life* as a writer of pamphlets, broadsides, periodical pieces, and, of course, his Journals. The childlike naïveté of this wonder is a bit startling in the opening to *Hypochondriack* no. 53, "On Words," written less than three years before Johnson died:

1. A fundamental misinterpretation of Boswell's attitude toward the past explains the wrongheadedness of Louis Baldwin in "The Conversation in Boswell's 'Life of Johnson,' " pp. 492–506. Baldwin seeks to show that Boswell did not, *pace* Pottle, have anything like total recall. As evidence of this, he points to repetitions and inconsistencies in Johnson's behavior that are not cross-referenced, and to Boswell's frequent apologies for his inadequate record-keeping. Actually, both matters indicate Boswell's desire to include as much as he can remember from the past: the need for cross-references does not occur to Boswell when his chief interest is recording as much Johnsoniana as possible, and his numerous apologies are the sincere self-chiding of a virtuoso who has temporarily fallen short of the high standards that he has set for himself.

> Words, the representations, or rather signs of ideas and notions in the human race, though habitual to all of us, are, when abstractly considered, exceedingly wonderful; in so much, that by endeavouring to think of them with a spirit of intense inquiry, I have been affected even with giddiness and a kind of stupor, the consequence of having one's faculties stretched in vain. I suppose this has been experienced by many of my readers, who in a fit of musing, have tried to trace the connection between a word of ordinary use and its meaning, repeating the word over and over again, and still starting in a kind of foolish amazement, as if listening for information from some secret power in the mind itself. [2]

Here is a dominant Boswellian trait, the love of turning something over in the mind until one's intellect staggers. Boswell's giddiness, his urge to muddle his mind by the excessive contemplation of insoluble problems, is self-destructive, a kind of death wish. This is the reason why he loves to view Johnson as ultimately mysterious and unknowable, and why, when he occasionally sees Johnson losing this aura, he is disappointed despite his awareness that this clarification is the necessary prelude to their deeper friendship. The tension between fact and interpretation (in the extreme, between barely relevant trivia and heavy-handed moralizing) in the *Life* is largely the result of Boswell's wavering between these two poles: Johnson as a mysterious, essentially unknowable entity, whose life can be recorded but not explained, and Johnson as a complex, though knowable person, whose behavior proceeds from certain fixed principles. Boswell's split view of this matter is analogous to, or perhaps engendered by, his own alternations between periods of compulsive orderliness and debilitating melancholia.

2. *Hypochondriack,* ed. Margery Bailey, 2: 150.

Various parts of this study have noted the oscillation in the *Life* between energy and lassitude, order and looseness, and interpretation and chronicle. The conclusion will explore the larger consequences of this Boswellian movement, and focus on two questions. What does the *Life* have in common with contemporary concepts of history and the past? And, to what extent did Boswell see the *Life* as the final word on Johnson?

The view that human nature has remained constant in all countries and throughout time, and that the study of history reveals certain abiding principles at work in human behavior, is called uniformitarianism. Its influence can be discerned among the numerous historiographical and philosophical schools of the neoclassical period. Since this view tends to ignore historical causation and to treat the past as a repository of moral examples or as a subject of antiquarian interest, history written from this perspective takes the forms of disconnected tableaux, chronicles, or propaganda dominated by an overriding idea, whether it be a religious or political bias or a rationalist's principle of universal behavior. Missing is any notion of man and nature developing through time. But this is the familiar side of this question.[3] What is more significant for our purposes is that many adherents of this view found a certain metaphor especially congenial for thinking about the past. This metaphor equates history (personal or collective) with a large space, which may be a vast darkened room or a sprawling plain. Since all past events inhabit this space, they are contemporaneous, coeval. This scheme is ahistorical and encourages the historian to group events

3. See R. G. Collingwood, *The Idea of History*, pp. 46–85; Herbert Davis, "The Augustan Conception of History"; and Stephen Toulmin and June Goodfield, *The Discovery of Time*, pp. 74–102.

topically, a practice that culminates in propaganda and escha-
tology.

The following excerpts are by no means an exhaustive
study of this metaphor's ramifications; they are instead an
introduction to its flexibility and the ways in which it in-
formed the neoclassical sense of the past. The first two passages are from Clarendon's *History of the Rebellion* (1702–
1704). In his dedication to Queen Anne, Clarendon combines
the metaphor with the hoary saw that history should instruct:

> By degrees your majesty is brought, in the course of this
> History, as it were *to the top of some exalted height, from
> whence you may behold all the errors and misfortunes of
> the time past* with advantage to yourself; *may view armies
> drawn up, and battles fought,* without your part of the
> danger; and, by the experience of former misfortunes,
> establish your own security.[4] [My italics]

Elsewhere, in his preface, Clarendon spatializes the past much
as Boswell does when he speaks of organizing his brushstrokes
into a portrait of Johnson; both men are thinking of the past
in terms of a spatial design. Clarendon here inveighs against
those who have been overly subtle in tracing the early causes
of the Civil Wars:

> *I shall not then lead any man farther back in this journey,
> for the discovery of the entrance into these dark ways,* than
> the beginning of this King's [Charles I] reign. For I am
> not so sharp-sighted as those who have discerned this rebel-
> lion contriving from, if not before, the death of Queen
> Elizabeth, and fomented by several Princes and great min-
> isters of state in Christendom to the time that it brake out.
> Neither do I look so far back as believing *the design to be*

4. Edward Hyde, Earl of Clarendon, *The History of the Rebellion
and Civil Wars in England,* ed. W. D. Macray, 3: lii.

so long since formed ... by viewing the temper, disposition, and habit, of that time, of the court and the country, we may discern the minds of men prepared, of some to do, and of others to suffer, all that hath since happened: the pride of this man, and the popularity of that; the levity of one, and the morosity of another; the excess of the court in the greatest want, and the parsimony and retention of the country in the greatest plenty; the spirit of craft and subtlety in some, and the rude and unpolished integrity of others, too much despising craft or art; *like so many atoms contributing jointly to this mass of confusion now before us.*[5] [My italics]

Notice what Clarendon has done here. First, although he is describing historical events, he gives us no sense of process; instead we have a great landscape with something here, something there, and so forth. Furthermore, although he is describing "this mass of confusion," he has rigidly ordered his details, mainly on the principle of contrast. With only minimal changes in wording, he could have shaken these details up into a random series, and the effect would have conveyed a more genuine sense of confusion. The grab-bag series of things that we find in Swift's prose are often of this sort. Clarendon has ordered these fragments in a way that does not strike us as especially chaotic because he has a double aim in this passage: he is saying, "the history of this period appears confused to you, but I can see that there is a general thrust, even a design, here." Clarendon has quietly blended two points of view, the layman's bewilderment and the historian's confidence.

There is a similar split in the *Life,* though Boswell wavers in his confidence that he can clarify matters for his readers. Clarendon orders his details much as Boswell frequently

5. Clarendon, 1: 3–4.

describes Johnson's qualities, showing how some traits are related to others and some are opposed (remember the Humean principles of association: temporal or spatial contiguity, cause and effect, and similarity or contrast). This observation of the world through a series of details arranged in a neat spatial pattern has been noted in Augustan poetry, linked with the popularity of prospect poems, and seen as fundamental to the "mode" of all the poetry of the period.[6]

Gibbon uses this metaphor more dramatically. The past is darkness into which the historian can throw some light; moreover, since he is speaking of his tremendous reading program before writing *The Decline and Fall,* Gibbon also sees his own mind as a dark space which he must illuminate with reference points.

> Such vague and multifarious reading [his childhood books] could not teach me to think, to write, or to act, and the only principle that *darted a ray of light into the indigested chaos* was an early and rational application to *the order of time and place.* The maps of Cellarius and Wells *imprinted in my mind the picture of ancient geography;* from Strauchius I imbibed the elements of chronology. The tables of Helvicus and Anderson, the annals of Usher and Prideaux, distinguished the connection of events, and I engraved the multitude of names and dates *in a clear and indelible series.*[7] [My italics]

6. Writing on Thomson's poem to Newton, Ralph Cohen, in "The Augustan Mode in English Poetry," observes that the "prospect view leading to a harmony of apparent or actual unity reflects the Augustan principle of a spatial world observed through successive details, the embracing unity of which is a form of spatial blending, that is, one detail fitting next to another like colors in a rainbow." Furthermore, "this blending leads to a momentary insight that gives the sense of a harmony, normally limited by the fragments from which a whole must be inferred" (p. 13).

7. Edward Gibbon, *Autobiography,* ed. Dero A. Saunders, p. 67.

> *The subsidiary rays of medals and inscriptions, of geog-*
> *raphy and chronology, were thrown on their proper objects.*
> *... Through the darkness of the Middle Ages I explored*
> *my way in the Annals and Antiquities of Italy of the*
> *learned Muratori, and diligently compared them with the*
> *parallel or transverse lines* of Sigonius and Maffei, Baronius
> and Pagi, till I almost grasped the ruins of Rome in the
> fourteenth century, without suspecting that this final chap-
> ter must be attained by the labor of six quartos and twenty
> years.[8] [My italics]

Although Gibbon's use of the metaphor deëmphasizes its
three-dimensionality, he nevertheless sees the past as a set of
events with eternally fixed relationships that can be discovered merely by casting the light of one's intellect in their
direction.

Although the spatializations of the past and of the mind
are logically separate metaphors, they are sometimes conflated, especially in discussions of memory like these excerpts
from Gibbon's *Autobiography*. Likening the mind in the act
of recall to a room or an expanse undoubtedly derives from
the ancient mnemonic device of using the mental image of an
articulated, precisely remembered space (such as one's own
house) and populating it with obvious cues to blocks of
learned matter that must be held in certain relationships. To
recall the material in its proper sequence, one need only walk
through this mental house and observe the objects in it. Originally this was a device for orators, and after a particular
speech had been delivered, the same house could be cleared
and used countless times afterward. From the Renaissance
through the eighteenth century, one of the most popular
spaces for this purpose was a theater, whose various parts,
including the aisles and rows of seats, provided a kind of grid

8. Gibbon, pp. 165–66.

for establishing many complex cross-connections.[9] In the passage quoted, Gibbon is concerned with creating just such a grid for himself before he passes on to the finer points of ancient history. Given the currency of this device in hundreds of treatises on the art of memory, it is easy to understand how the mind-as-a-space image became one of the root metaphors of the neoclassical age; indeed, it is still with us, though its implications have changed somewhat. During the Enlightenment, the metaphor predisposed investigators of human nature to lay out their schemes with an order and symmetry that is rather embarrassing today. Hume, for instance, in *An Inquiry Concerning Human Understanding*, asserts that the validity of his enterprise, which he calls "this mental geography," is based on the philosopher's ability "to know the different operations of the mind, to separate them from each other, to class them under their proper heads, and to correct all that seeming disorder in which they lie involved."[10]

Boswell, too, sees the mind as a large, subdivided space. Sometimes the subdivisions of this mental space represent a summary of the lessons that experience has taught him: in this manner he reduces his past to a group of rooms:

> We went at night to the inn on Barnby Moor. We were now jumbled into old acquaintance. I felt myself quite strong, and exulted when I compared my present mind with my mind some years ago. *Formerly my mind was quite a lodging-house for all ideas who chose to put up there,* so that it was at the mercy of accident, for I had no fixed mind of my own. *Now my mind is a house where, though the street rooms and the upper floors are open to strangers, yet there is always a settled family in the back parlour and*

9. See Frances A. Yates, *The Art of Memory*.

10. David Hume, *An Inquiry Concerning Human Understanding* [1748], ed. Charles W. Hendel, sec. 1, p. 22.

sleeping-closet behind it; and this family can judge of the ideas which come to lodge. This family! this landlord, let me say, or this landlady, as the mind and the soul are both she. I shall confuse myself with metaphor. Let me then have done with it. Only this more. *The ideas—my lodgers —are of all sorts.* Some, gentlemen of the law, who pay me a great deal more than others. Divines of all sorts have been with me, and have ever [even?] disturbed me. *When I first took up house,* Presbyterian ministers used to make me melancholy with dreary tones. Methodists next shook my passions. Romish clergy filled me with solemn ideas, and, although their statues and many movable ornaments are gone, *yet they drew some pictures upon my walls* with such deep strokes that they still remain. They are, indeed, only agreeable ones. I had Deists for a very short while. But they, being sceptics, were perpetually alarming me with *thoughts that my walls were made of clay and could not last,* so I was glad to get rid of them. I am forced to own that *my rooms have been occupied by women of the town,* and by some ladies of abandoned manners. But I am resolved that by degrees *there shall be only decent people and innocent, gay lodgers.*[11] [My italics]

Sometimes the subdivisions of this mental space represent the categories of the old faculty psychology, as in this shrewd analysis of Johnson:

His mind resembled the vast amphitheatre, the Colisaeum at Rome. In the centre stood his judgment, which, like a

11. *Boswell in Search of a Wife, 1766–1769,* eds. Frank Brady and Frederick A. Pottle, pp. 137–38. Notice here, by the way, the manifestations of several previously mentioned Boswellian traits: a lack of personal identity, a persistent but frail determination to remedy his backsliding, a fondness for stretching comparisons to their limits, and a horror of philosophical and religious skepticism.

mighty gladiator, combated those apprehensions that, *like the wild beasts of the Arena, were all around in cells, ready to be let out upon him. After a conflict, he drove them back into their dens;* but not killing them, they were still assailing him. [26 Oct. 1769; my italics][12]

One final passage illustrates how this spatialization of the past can be self-consciously explored by a master of logic and imagery, Samuel Johnson:

> If the most active and industrious of mankind was able, at the close of life, to recollect distinctly his past moments, and distribute them, in a regular account, according to the manner in which they have been spent, it is scarcely to be imagined how few would be marked out to the mind, by any permanent or visible effects, how small a proportion his real action would bear to his seeming possibilities of action, *how many chasms he would find of wide and continued vacuity, and how many interstitial spaces unfilled,* even in the most tumultuous hurries of business, and the most eager vehemence of pursuit.
>
>   *It is said by modern philosophers, that not only the great globes of matter are thinly scattered thro' the universe, but the hardest bodies are so porous, that, if all matter were compressed to perfect solidity, it might be contained in a cube of a few feet. In a like manner, if all the employment of life were crowded into the time which it really occupied, perhaps a few weeks, days, or hours, would be sufficient for*

12. It is possible that this amphitheatre is a conscious variation on the lodging house metaphor, since the Journal entry is for 20 March 1768 and the passage from the *Life* covers 26 October 1769. In the laborious process of transforming his Journal into Johnson's biography, Boswell probably reread the lodging house passage shortly before he wrote the entries in the *Life* for 1769.

its accomplishment, so far as the mind was engaged in the performance.[13] [My italics]

Of course, the eighteenth century was not unique in its tendency to think of the past in spatial terms; we are still prone to locate all our memories (particularly the quieter, less significant ones) in a large room and to place all the actors on the same stage until we have made a conscious effort to sort out these old scenes into their proper sequence. Once we have done this, however, we have obscured the associations that we have at least unconsciously made among these events. To look for trends, patterns, and meanings in our past often requires us to go back to where we started before we had established the proper chronological order of mental images. But we are not merely putting Humpty Dumpty back to-

13. Samuel Johnson, *Rambler*, no. 8; in *Selected Essays from the Rambler, Adventurer, and Idler*, ed. W. J. Bate, pp. 21–22. It is a commonplace that neoclassical prose and poetry, especially Johnson's, are devoid of imagery in their pursuit of general truths. This is a misrepresentation deriving in part from the eighteenth century's revulsion at the literary excesse of the previous age, those of the Metaphysical poets in particular. In " 'Pictures to the Mind': Johnson and Imagery," Donald J. Greene champions Johnson as a friend of imagery. He points to the importance of "imagery" and "imagination" as criteria for value judgments in *Lives of the Poets*, and to the imagery in Johnson's poem "On the Death of Mr. Robert Levet" as well as in the genuinely metaphysical poem "To Miss Carpenter, on Her Playing upon the Harpsichord in a Room hung with some Flower-pieces of her own Painting." Boswell, too, delighted in lively imagery, and especially in striking similes. In his Journals he sometimes indulges his fancy, spinning out a comparison to its limits. *Boswell on the Grand Tour: Germany and Switzerland, 1764:* ideas are like flowers (p. 65). *Boswell on the Grand Tour: Italy, Corsica, and France 1765–1766:* a garden is like a spread periwig (p. 77). *Boswell in Search of A Wife 1766–1769:* his mind is like a house (pp. 137–38); a rich man is like a fat man (p. 222); breakfast is like fortification (p. 306). *Boswell for The Defence, 1769–1774:* an actor is like a barrister (p. 17); London life is like a banquet (p. 61); life is like a monotonous journal of the weather (p. 222); the mind is like a crude stereopticon (p. 265).

gether again. Our firmer knowledge of the sequence of events provides us with a caveat in our search for meaning: because we are all developing and evolving at different rates and in different ways, a man's actions at two separate points in time may have the same face value and yet involve different motives and character traits. For this reason, the historian, biographer, or autobiographer cannot sort out the events in men's and nations' lives as blithely as he would the suits in a deck of cards.

Unlike Hawkins, Boswell never reduces Johnson to a rigid pattern of traits; however, his assurance that some design was there allowed him to appeal to it without ever fully articulating it. We are thus led to share Boswell's sense of Johnson's monumental integrity, a feat made possible by Boswell's habit of reifying his experience, of labeling parts of his past and treating them like building blocks in the great edifice of "James Boswell" or "Samuel Johnson." This tendency is typical of the neoclassical period. Today, we are much more likely to preserve in our language the experiential nature of our past moments. Boswell, for example, reifies friendship, referring to it as an object to be possessed, maintained, or lost; today, however, we should probably say "He is my friend" rather than "I have his friendship." Indeed, the latter is no longer even a viable linguistic alternative in informal discourse. As a result of this change, "friendship" has become for us an increasingly abstract noun, to be reserved for philosophical, religious, or sociological discussions. Similarly, Boswell often reifies the act of conversation, as can be seen in the *Life,* where, as a rule, he looks back on past convivialities chiefly for the good things to be extracted from them. In this way, with a few notable exceptions, Boswell's recorded conversations tend to be collections of anecdotes, not a series of dramatic events.

Because of this reification of friendship and conversation,

the *Life* typically fragments not into scenes or subplots but into topics, virtues, traits and memorable sayings, all of which may be grouped to violate chronology. Boswell offers many of the details of the *Life* as new building blocks in the monument or new brushstrokes in the portrait; in either case, the noble and imposing stasis (not a strict consistency) of Johnson the man has been reinforced.

We have seen that Boswell's fondness for different points of view does not stem from cynicism concerning the existence of an absolute truth. He hopes that the real Johnson resides somewhere in his mountain of Johnsoniana. His relativism is that of an agnostic rather than an atheist. His humility in this matter leads him to document sources at the expense of narrative grace, but his awareness of analogies, similarities, and dissimilarities often makes him treat his materials as individual blocks that can be juggled until he finds their proper place. Reinforcing his tendency to do this was his method of composition, which forced him to reshuffle papers that frequently were inconsistent, overlapped, or remained silent about long stretches of Johnson's life.

Boswell's outlook, like that of his contemporaries, is still essentially medieval: essence precedes existence.[14] The man or age that does not understand the complexities of historical development or experiential change displays a naïve readiness to draw parallels between two moments in time. Bos-

14. In "The Substantive Level," *The Verbal Icon*, pp. 140–41, Wimsatt points the connection between "the denial of proper essences or species" and "the victory in short of the phenomenal over the noumenal, of qualities over things." It is significant that Boswell's prime innovation in biography, his recorded conversations, are the result of his desire to portray more of Johnson's existential complexity than he can in a character analysis. That Boswell sometimes relates and cross-references his passages like an old believer in essences and at other times takes refuge in the concrete and the accidental is merely another narrative technique that reminds us of temporal restlessness of the *Life* and helps us see Boswell as a transitional figure.

well's personal tragedy is that he was never able to reify himself, as Johnson, through great personal struggles, was able to do. Boswell thrilled to the heady variety of his experience and yet sought for the permanence beneath it.

Since Boswell was so impressed with Johnson's integrity and since he tried so diligently to put all the pieces together, did he regard the *Life*, the product of his labors, as a provisional or a definitive portrait? This question does not quite yield itself to an either-or solution. The attempt to write a history becomes in Boswell's case intensely frustrating because he shared Johnson's faith in the worth of all knowledge.[15] Despite the firm commitment of English biography to didacticism, Boswell indulged his penchant for inclusiveness in the *Life* at the expense of relatively simplistic generalizations; indeed, his wavering between inclusiveness and commentary is what generates the temporal restlessness and mixture of styles in the work. He does not settle on a fixed point of view because his respect for Johnson and his reverential awe for the mysterious complexity of Johnson's personality made him want to portray his various sides as completely as possible.

The departure from earlier biographical methods that Boswell's inclusiveness represents may be linked to eighteenth-century editorial practices, which reveal a growing reluctance to emend Homer, Virgil, Chaucer, or Shakespeare merely because a passage appeared unworthy of them. Since the older rules refused to acknowledge that a master may nod, "inferior" passages were treated as subsequent interpolations or corruptions of the original version. The newer and more cautious editorial attitudes and Boswell's hetero-

15. See John Hardy, "Johnson and Raphael's Counsel to Adam." Hardy cites *Rambler* no. 83; *Life*, 1 July 1763 and 14 April 1775; and *Letters*, no. 944.

geneous biography of Johnson are both based on a more realistic grasp of the complexity of the human character.[16] To be more precise, the new trends, based on a growing awareness of the restricting artificiality of certain literary conventions, reveal a conviction that one may set down in words the contradictions in a man's personality without unleashing chaos. Thus, what the wisest always knew to be so in life came to be accepted in literature.

To counterbalance the almost self-indulgent inclusiveness of the *Life,* Boswell has seen to it that a piece of Johnsoniana can almost always be put into its proper perspective. If he is making a large point, such as Johnson's kindness to people, he usually states what he is trying to demonstrate. If the detail is a small one, a tossed-off quip that is somewhat cruel or a brief critical judgment that seems narrow-minded, then these matters generally reside in a welter of Johnsonian tidbits whose very number becomes self-corrective, demonstrating that Johnson's qualities in an informal talk may swing one way or another while his real nature lies somewhere in between.

We can now tell from an examination of Boswell's Private Papers that he did not use many of the details that his contributors gave him. Though it at first appears that he is whitewashing his great friend's odd social behavior, insanity, excesses at the table, mean-mindedness, profanity, use of drugs, and so on, nevertheless all of these weaknesses are mentioned in the *Life,* but not dwelt upon.[17] After all, the *Life* was an attempt to repair Johnson's reputation after the sallies of Mrs. Piozzi and Sir John Hawkins. It appears that

16. See, for instance, Johnson's preface to his edition of Shakespeare: "To alter is more easy than to explain, and temerity is a more common quality than diligence."

17. Boswell's editorial practices are treated by Marshall Waingrow in his introduction to *Correspondence . . . Relating to the Making of the Life of Johnson,* pp. xxv–xliv.

Boswell's motive in omitting certain details was compounded of a desire to suppress unpleasant Johnsoniana and to strike the proper overall proportion between the man's virtues and vices. To include too many anecdotes illustrating Johnson's bearishness, for instance, would be to falsify the greater reality of the man. The guidance that Boswell gives his reader is an attempt to compromise, to communicate his view of Johnson without limiting others' interpretations of him, in the event that their insights go beyond those offered in the *Life*. This delicate balance is much like that between the "foreseen" and the "fortuitous" that Sutherland has noted in some neoclassical prose.[18] In more general terms, these tensions are between authority and surprise, stability and quirkiness, the elements that fit into a scheme and those that do not.

Since Boswell himself does not always maintain this balance between authority and humility, it is not surprising that some readers of the *Life* respond accordingly by overrating or underrating the judgment and understanding in this view of Johnson. Two recent essays, appearing in the same collection, illustrate these extremes. Ralph W. Rader, in an article that brilliantly analyzes the famous Johnson-Wilkes encounter at Dilly's, is guilty of investing Boswell with too much perspicacity and self-conscious literary craftsmanship. Rader begins with the Aristotelian dictum that "literary pleasure results from the vivid representation to our consciousness of striking human acts, morally determinate, which move us through our perception of the internal probability and ethical consonance of their inception, continuance, and completion."[19] He adds that Boswell renders the acts in the *Life* "vivid and striking, makes us see them as

18. See chap. 4, n. 4.
19. Ralph W. Rader, "Literary Form in Factual Narrative: The Example of Boswell's *Johnson*," p. 18.

internally probable in terms of motive and circumstance, and adjusts our view so that we always see them as ethically consonant both in themselves and with the morally determinant image of an admirable Johnson."[20] This is a fruitful startingpoint for an analysis of the *Life*. Boswell did have an atemporal image of Johnson in his mind; it is for this reason that he uses the *Life*-as-a-portrait metaphor so easily and often. This image, as Rader shows, does condition Boswell's use of his materials, so that the *Life*, as Saintsbury remarks, is continuously entertaining but not the sort of book that compels us to read on and on. However, Rader exaggerates a bit the doggedness with which Boswell tailored the *Life* to fit the image. There are so many Boswellian motives behind the writing of the *Life* that we can sometimes only guess which ones are operative in a given passage; certainly it is difficult to assert that Boswell "always proportions his treatment of a fact to the relevance it has for the image of essential character."[21] Boswell only suspected Johnson's essence; he could not afford to be dogmatic—he says as much when he justifies the inclusion of apparent trivia in the *Life*. A reader of the *Life* is led by Boswell to grope for this essence, to sense a coherence and to piece the man together. Boswell sees this process as an ongoing one: he is as humble before the mystery of Johnson's personality as he is before his own.

Radically disagreeing with Rader is Donald J. Greene in an essay which is primarily a long-overdue plea for the study of eighteenth-century autobiography. Greene sees the portrait of Johnson in the *Life* as hopelessly marred by Boswell's intrusions and the lack of objectivity which led him into numerous distortions.[22] Unlike Rader, therefore, Greene sees

20. Ibid.
21. Rader, p. 14.
22. Donald J. Greene, "The Uses of Autobiography in the Eighteenth Century," pp. 52, 56–58.

Boswell as sadly cut off from Johnson's essence, or larger significance. Greene maintains that a reader of autobiographies has, through the tone of the writing and its other idiosyncrasies, immediate access to the deeper parts of the author's personality in a way that a reader of biographies does not.[23] While this is undoubtedly true, especially for an in-depth study of a man, there are two objections to the claim. First of all, if an intelligent reader of an autobiography understands the tone and the man's more personal thoughts, he can then proceed to write a biography, including his insights as well as the details that resist analysis. Second, few men are capable of seeing themselves as others see them, so that a good biographer, though admittedly handicapped by his ignorance of thousands of private thoughts and emotional states, can nevertheless place his man in perspective, showing how he was greeted and judged by his peers and the rest of the external world. Surely, part of a man's "meaning" depends on this outside view.

Boswell's oscillation between public and private views of Johnson is frequently rapid and dramatically effective; only occasionally is it merely awkward. Indeed, this movement, together with the tension between facts and interpretation, generates what we have called the narrative's temporal restlessness, which in turn is reflected by the variety of styles in the *Life*. In the last analysis, the elements of Boswell's style are unidiosyncratic; what makes the *Life* unique is his rather desperate attempt to have it both ways, to include all available materials for posterity's continued study and to interpret everything to the best of his ability.[24] Although each of these

23. Greene, p. 51.
24. Of course, the biographer, whose subject is a man, can include far more contingent, or only obliquely relevant, material than can the novelist, whose accidental details are only relatively contingent since they are usually subsumed by his theme(s). The novelist's plight here is discussed by Martin Price in "The Other Self: Thoughts about Character in the Novel."

mutually exclusive goals is many times temporarily neglected in the *Life,* the energy with which Boswell pursues both of them is what makes him stand out from the other biographers and historians of his time.

Many twentieth-century readers are annoyed by the *Life* because it offers them a monolithic hero in a conglomerate structure; the fullness of the record prevents them from "getting their bearings" in Johnson's life story. Boswell's interpretation is personal, limited, provisional, and open-ended. The tidier form of novels and other biographies reflects the author's resolution of certain problems concerning his subject and narrative method. Sensing this authorial confidence, we find it relatively easy to assign these books an unambiguous role in our emotional lives. Once we are comfortable with the coherence or simple ambivalence of our reactions (even paradox is, to some degree, a resolution of the world's complexity), the power of actuality in these books has been somewhat neutralized so that they can be conveniently stored in our memories, to be recalled at appropriate moments, or perhaps not at all. The *Life* is recalcitrant matter which resists this process. Long after we have put the work aside, its amiable mixture of the general and the concrete becomes teasingly and unpredictably present in our minds, and it is always disconcerting when books insist this way on spilling over into our lives.

APPENDIX ONE: *Narrative Topics in the*
                     Life *before 1763*

For the purposes of this list, page references are more accurate than dates. The pages given are all in volume 1 of the Hill-Powell edition of the *Life*. Note that much of this early part of the *Life* is an elaborate list of Johnson's works, as the repetition of the heading "Johnson's writings" indicates.

APPENDIX TWO: *The Number of Days*
(by Year) That Boswell
Saw Johnson and the
Dates of Their Meetings,
as Recorded in the Life

Meetings not dated in the
Life are given below in brackets; the dates are derived from
P. A. W. Collins, "Boswell's Contact with Johnson," *Notes
and Queries* 201 (1956): 163–66. Revising Croker's figures,
Collins estimates that Boswell saw Johnson on about 425 days
in all. Collins also points out that Boswell met Johnson more
frequently in the later years of their friendship, estimating
that, after 1772, they saw each other 40–45 percent of the days
when they were within reach.

1763   *21 days:* May 16, 24; June 13, [ca. 15], 25; July 1, 5, 6, 9,
        14, 19, 20, 21, 26, 28, 30, 31; August 2, 3, 5, 6
1766   *3 days:* February [12], 15, [22]
1768   *8 days:* March [26], [27], [28]; May [2], [ca. 18], [24],
        [29], [30]
1769   *10 days:* September [ca. 28], 30; October 6, 10, 16, 19,
        20, 26, 27; November 10
1772   *17 days:* March 21, 23, 28, 31; April 5, 6, 9, 10, 11, 15,
        17, 18, 19, [22], [24], [28]; May 9
1773   *15 days:* April 3, 8, 9, 11, 13, 15, 19, 21, 27, 29, 30; May

1, 7, 9, 10. Also in this year were eighty-eight consecutive days (August 14 to November 22) which Boswell wrote up in his *Journal of a Tour to the Hebrides.*

1775   *22 days:* March 21, 24, 27, 28, 31; April 1, 2, 5, 6, 7, 8, 10, 13, 14, 16, 18; May 6, [ca. 7], 8, 12, 13, 17

1776   *49+ days:* March 16, 18, 19, 20, 21, 22, 23, 24, 25, 26, 27, 28, 29, 31; April 3, 4, 5, 7, 10, 11, 12, 29; May [5], [7], [8], [9], [10], [12], [13], 15, 16. In addition there is a short section of undated sayings from the period between April 12 and April 29, at Bath.

1777   *10 days:* September 14, 15, 16, 17, 19, 20, 21, 22, 23, 24

1778   *31 days:* March 18, 20, 30, 31; April 3, 4, 7, 8, 9, 10, 12, 13, 14, 15, 17, 18, 19, 20, 25, 28, 29, 30; May 2, 8, 9, 10, 12, 13, 16, 17, 19

1779   *18+ days:* March 16, 26, 29, 31; April 1, 2, 3, 4, 7, 8, 16, 24, 26; May 1, 3; October 4, 10, 12. Additions might be made during the periods March 26–29 and October 4–10, when Boswell was negligent in recording; there is a short section of undated sayings following October 12.

1781   *18+ days:* March 20, 21, [26], [28], 30; April 1, 6, 7, 12, 13, 15, 20; May 8, 17; June 2, 3, 4, 5. In addition there is a diffuse narrative covering late May.

1783   *16+ days:* March 21, 22, 23, 30, [31]; April 10, 12, 18, 20, 28, 30; May 1, 15, [ca. 24], 26, 29. In addition there is a long section of undated sayings for early April.

1784   *25+days:* May 6, [ca. 8], 9, 10, 15, 16, 17, 18, 19, 30; June 3, 9, 10, 11, 12, 13, 14?, 15, 16, 22, 23, 24, 25, 27, 30. In addition there is a long section of undated sayings between June 16 and June 22.

Outlines of Hypochondriack No. 1 and No. 2, with Paragraph Divisions Indicated

Hypochondriack No. 1

I. Periodical form an advantage to writers and readers
  A. Advantage to writers
    1. Writing a large book
    2. Writing a short essay
      a) advantage to "men of greatest parts and application"
      b) advantage to less accomplished men
        ¶
  B. Advantage to readers
    1. Greater, more exquisite variety in small things
    2. Application of previous arguments (2a, 2b) to readers also
      ¶
  C. Recapitulation: periodical form of mutual benefit
      ¶
II. Periodical of British origin: Britain's are best, despite spread to many countries
      ¶

III. Good reception expected for *The Hypochondriack* in England, where hypochondria is so common
   A. This opinion verified by foreigners: Britain, "the gloomy isle"
      1. Hypochondria, however, not peculiar to Britain
      2. Boswell's desire to remedy, not describe, the malady
   B. Boswell's credentials for discussing the sickness (he has had it but is now better)
      1. His general purpose, to divert; no correspondents desired
      2. Series of essays to be begun in gloomy November

Hypochondriack No. 2

  I. Fear as man's greatest suffering
      ¶
 II. Boasted fearlessness really affectation or insensibility
   A. Two examples [neither is an example of affectation]
   B. Examples of insensibility probably numerous [but Boswell gives none][1]
   C. Examples of affectation [six in five sentences]
      1. Sidetracked on Blair and Hervey's meditations
      2. Rather irrelevant example of schoolboy
      ¶
III. Fear necessary in human nature; not only unavoidable but also a corrective of human suffering [a barely coherent sentence]
      ¶
   A. Aristotle: pity and fear purge the passions
      ¶
   B. Fear a remedy for disorder of the passions; fear as a teacher of moderation
      ¶

1. In her edition of *The Hypochondriack* (1: 112*n*), Margery Bailey points out that Boswell later finds an example and "tucks it into his remarks upon the irrationality of armsmakers" in No. 3.

IV. Religious fear[2]

¶

V. Essay's original aim to caution readers against indulgence of unnecessary fear

¶

   A. Advice against habitually contemplating the possible evils that may beset us[3]

---

2. Boswell makes distinctions and then blurs them with the assertion that each man's personal devotion is necessarily different.

3. "The bitter potion is taken soon enough when we are obliged to take it."

BIBLIOGRAPHY

Addison, Joseph, Richard Steele, and others. *The Spectator*. Edited by
Donald F. Bond. 5 vols. Oxford: Clarendon Press, 1965.

Baldwin, Louis. "The Conversation in Boswell's 'Life of Johnson.'"
JEGP 51 (1952): 492–506.

Beardsley, Monroe C. *Aesthetics: Problems in the Philosophy of Criticism*.
New York: Harcourt, Brace, 1958.

Blair, Hugh. *Lectures in Rhetoric and Belles Lettres* [1783]. Edited by
Harold F. Harding. 2 vols. Carbondale, Illinois: Southern Illinois University Press, 1965.

Booth, Wayne C. "Distance and Point-of-View: An Essay in Classification." *Essays in Criticism* 11 (1961): 60–79.

Boswell, James. *Life of Samuel Johnson, LL.D.* 2 vols. London: printed
by H. Baldwin for C. Dilly, 1791. 2d edition, 3 vols., London: printed
by H. Baldwin for C. Dilly, 1793. 3d edition, 4 vols., London: C. Dilly,
1799. Later important editions: Edmond Malone, 1811; J. W. Croker,
1831, 1835, 1848; Percy Fitzgerald, 1874, 1900; Alexander Napier, 1884;
and Roger Ingpen, 1907. The definitive edition, which has been used
for this study, is by G. B. Hill 6 vols., Oxford: Clarendon Press, 1887,
revised by L. F. Powell, 1934–1950. A one-volume edition in the Oxford Standard Authors series, Oxford 1933, has an introduction by
C. B. Tinker; the text was revised by R. W. Chapman, 1953.

———. *Letters of James Boswell*. Edited by Chauncey Brewster Tinker.
2 vols. Oxford: Clarendon Press 1924.

———. *The Hypochondriack*. Edited by Margery Bailey. 2 vols. Stanford, California: Stanford University Press, 1928.

———. *Private Papers of James Boswell from Malahide Castle in the
Collection of Lt.-Colonel Ralph Heyward Isham*. Edited by Geoffrey
Scott and Frederick A. Pottle. 18 vols. Mount Vernon, New York: privately printed by W. E. Rudge, 1928–1934. The catalogue, edited by
Frederick A. and Marion S. Pottle, was published by the Oxford University Press, New York, 1931.

———. *Boswell's Journal of a Tour to the Hebrides with Samuel Johnson, LL.D. Now First Published from the Original Manuscript.* Edited by Frederick A. Pottle and Charles H. Bennett, New York: Viking Press, 1936. New edition with additional notes by F. A. Pottle, New York: McGraw-Hill, 1961.

———. *Boswell's London Journal, 1762–1763.* Edited by Frederick A. Pottle. New York: McGraw-Hill, 1950.

———. *Boswell in Holland, 1763–1764.* Edited by Frederick A. Pottle. New York: McGraw-Hill, 1952.

———. *Boswell on the Grand Tour: Germany and Switzerland, 1764.* Edited by Frederick A. Pottle. New York: McGraw-Hill, 1953.

———. *Boswell on the Grand Tour: Italy, Corsica and France, 1765–1766.* Edited by Frank Brady and Frederick A. Pottle. New York: McGraw-Hill, 1955.

———. *Boswell in Search of a Wife, 1766–1769.* Edited by Frank Brady and Frederick A. Pottle. New York: McGraw-Hill, 1956.

———. *Boswell for the Defence, 1769–1774.* Edited by William, K. Wimsatt, Jr., and Frederick A. Pottle. New York: McGraw-Hill, 1959.

———. *Boswell: The Ominous Years, 1774–1776.* Edited by Charles Ryskamp and Frederick A. Pottle. New York: McGraw-Hill, 1963.

———. *Boswell in Extremes, 1776–1778.* Edited by Charles McC. Weis and Frederick A. Pottle. New York: McGraw-Hill, 1970.

———. *The Correspondence of James Boswell and John Johnston of Grange.* Edited by R. S. Walker. New York: McGraw-Hill, 1966.

———. *The Correspondence and Other Papers of James Boswell Relating to the Making of the Life of Johnson.* Edited by Marshall Waingrow. New York: McGraw-Hill, 1969.

———. "Boswell's London Journal of 1778." Edited by Inge Probstein. Ph.D. dissertation, Yale University, 1951.

Bronson, Bertrand. "Personification Reconsidered." *ELH* 14 (1947): 163–77.

———. *Johnson Agonistes and Other Essays.* Berkeley and Los Angeles: University of California Press, 1965. Reprint of University of California Publications in English, vol. 3, no. 9 (1944), and of "The Double Tradition of Dr. Johnson," *ELH* 18 (1951): 90–106.

Butt, John. *Biography in the Hands of Walton, Johnson and Boswell.* Los Angeles: University of California Press, 1966.

Carlyle, Thomas. *Critical and Miscellaneous Essays.* New York: J. B. Alden, 1885.

Carroll, John B. "Vectors of Prose Style." In *Style in Language,* edited by T. A. Sebeok. Cambridge: M.I.T. Press, 1960.

Cibber, Theophilus. *Lives of the Poets.* 5 vols. London, 1753.

Cohen, Ralph. *The Art of Discrimination: Thomson's The Seasons and the Language of Criticism.* Berkeley and Los Angeles: University of California Press, 1964.

―――. "The Augustan Mode in English Poetry." *Eighteenth-Century Studies* 1 (1967): 3–32.

Collingwood, R. G. *The Idea of History.* Oxford: Clarendon Press, 1946.

Collins, P. A. W. "Boswell's Contact with Johnson." *Notes and Queries* 201 (1956): 163–66.

Davis, Herbert. "The Augustan Conception of History." In *Reason and the Imagination: Studies in the History of Ideas, 1600–1800,* edited by J. A. Mazzeo. New York: Columbia University Press, 1962.

Fielding, Henry. *Works.* Edited by W. E. Henley. 16 vols. London, 1903.

Fifer, C. N. "Boswell and the Decorous Bishop." *JEGP* 61 (1962): 48–56.

Fitzgerald, Percy. *Boswell's Autobiography.* London: Chatto & Windus, 1912.

Frank, Joseph. "Spatial Form in Modern Literature." *Sewanee Review* 53 (1945): 221–40, 433–56, 643–53.

Frye, Northrop. *The Well-Tempered Critic.* Bloomington: Indiana University Press, 1963.

Fuller, Thomas. *The History of the Worthies of England* [1662]. Edited by P. Austin Nuttall. 3 vols. London: Tegg, 1840.

Fussell, Paul, Jr. "The Force of Literary Memory in Boswell's *London Journal.*" *Studies in English Literature* 2 (1962): 351–57.

Gibbon, Edward. *The Autobiography of Edward Gibbon.* Edited by Dero A. Saunders. New York: Meridian Books, 1961.

Goldstein, Harvey D. *"Ut Poesis Pictura:* Reynolds on Imitation and Imagination." *Eighteenth-Century Studies* 1 (1968): 213–35.

Gordon, Ian A. *The Movement of English Prose.* London: Longmans, 1966.

Greene, Donald J. " 'Pictures to the Mind': Johnson and Imagery." In *Johnson, Boswell and Their Circle: Essays Presented to L. F. Powell.* Oxford: Clarendon Press, 1965.

―――. "The Uses of Autobiography in the Eighteenth Century." In *Essays in Eighteenth-Century Biography,* edited by Philip B. Daghlian. Bloomington: Indiana University Press, 1968.

Haller, William. *The Rise of Puritanism.* New York: Columbia University Press, 1938.

Hardy, John. "Johnson and Raphael's Counsel to Adam." In *Johnson, Boswell and Their Circle: Essays Presented to L. F. Powell.* Oxford: Clarendon Press, 1965.

Hart, Francis R. "Boswell and the Romantics: A Chapter in the History of Biographical Theory." *ELH* 27 (1960): 44–65.

Hart, Jeffrey. "Some Thoughts on Johnson as Hero." In *Johnsonian Studies,* edited by Magdi Wahba. Cairo: Société Orientale de Publicité, 1962.

Hawkins, Sir John. *The Life of Samuel Johnson, LL.D.* [1787]. Edited and abridged by Bertram H. Davis. New York: Macmillan & Co., 1961.

Hay, James, ed. *Johnson: His Characteristics and Aphorisms*. London: A. Gardner, 1884.

Hill, George Birkbeck. *Dr. Johnson: His Friends and His Critics*. London: 1870.

————, ed. *Johnsonian Miscellanies*. 2 vols. Oxford: Clarendon Press, 1897.

Hogarth, William. *The Analysis of Beauty, Written with a view of fixing the fluctuating Ideas of Taste* [1753]. Edited by Joseph Burke. Oxford: Clarendon Press, 1955.

Hume, David. *A Treatise of Human Nature* [1739–1740]. Edited by L. A. Selby-Bigge. Oxford: Clarendon Press, 1888.

————. *An Inquiry Concerning Human Understanding* [1748]. Edited by Charles W. Hendel. New York and Indianapolis: Liberal Arts Press, 1955.

Hurd, Richard. *Letters on Chivalry and Romance* [1762]. Edited by Hoyt Trowbridge. Los Angeles: William Andrews Clark Memorial Library (Augustan Reprint Society), 1963.

Hyde, Donald and Mary. "Dr. Johnson's Second Wife." In *New Light on Dr. Johnson,* edited by F. W. Hilles. New Haven: Yale University Press, 1959.

Hyde, Edward, Earl of Clarendon. *The History of the Rebellion and Civil Wars in England*. Edited by W. Dunn Macray. 6 vols. Oxford: Clarendon Press, 1888.

Johnson, Samuel. *Selected Essays from the Rambler, Adventurer, and Idler*. Edited by W. J. Bate. New Haven: Yale University Press, 1968.

————. *Lives of the English Poets* [1783; previously published as individual prefaces, 1779–1781]. Edited by George Birkbeck Hill. 3 vols. Oxford: Clarendon Press, 1905.

————. *Prayers and Meditations, Composed by Samuel Johnson, LL.D.* Collected by Rev. George Strahan. London, 1785.

Langbaine, Gerard. *Account of the English Dramatic Poets*. Oxford, 1691.

Lee, Rensselaer W. *"Ut Pictura Poesis." The Art Bulletin* 22 (1940): 197–269. Reprinted, New York: W. W. Norton, 1967.

Macaulay, Thomas B. "Samuel Johnson." In *Critical and Historical Essays,* edited by Hugh Trevor-Roper. New York: McGraw-Hill, 1965.

Mason, E. T., ed. *Johnson: His Words and His Ways. What He Did, and What Men Thought and Spoke Concerning Him*. New York: Harper & Bros., 1879.

Mason, William. *The Poems of Mr. Gray, to Which Are Prefixed Memoirs of His Life and Writings by W. Mason, M.A.* York, 1775.

Middleton, Conyers. *The Life and Letters of Marcus Tullius Cicero* [1741]. London: H. G. Bohn, 1848.

Milic, Louis T. "Unconscious Ordering in the Prose of Swift." In *The Computer and Literary Style,* edited by Jacob Leed. Kent, Ohio: Kent State University Press, 1966.

Molin, Sven Eric. "Boswell's Account of the Johnson-Wilkes Meeting." *Studies in English Literature* 3 (1963): 307–22.

Moore, Robert E. "Reynolds and the Art of Characterization." In *Studies in Criticism and Aesthetics: Essays in Honor of Samuel Holt Monk.* Minneapolis: University of Minnesota Press, 1967.

Morrissette, Bruce. "The Evolution of Narrative Viewpoint in Robbe-Grillet." *Novel: A Forum on Fiction* 1 (1967): 24–33.

[Murray, John.] "Boswell and His Ego: Some Bicentenary Reflections. A Reputation Redressed." *Times Literary Supplement,* 26 October 1940, p. 545.

Novarr, David. *The Making of Walton's Lives.* Ithaca, New York: Cornell University Press, 1958.

Osborn, James M. "Edmond Malone and Dr. Johnson." In *Johnson, Boswell and Their Circle: Essays Presented to L. F. Powell.* Oxford: Clarendon Press, 1965.

Piozzi, Hester Lynch (Mrs. Thrale). *Anecdotes of Johnson* [1786]. Edited by S. C. Roberts. Cambridge: Cambridge University Press, 1932.

Postgate, R. W., ed. *The Conversations of Dr. Johnson, Selected from the "Life" by James Boswell.* New York: Vanguard Press, 1930.

Pottle, Frederick A. *The Literary Career of James Boswell Esq.* Oxford: Clarendon Press, 1929, 1966.

———. "Boswell's Shorthand." *Times Literary Supplement,* 28 July 1932, p. 545.

———. "The Power of Memory in Boswell and Scott." In *Essays on the Eighteenth Century Presented to D. Nichol Smith.* Oxford: Clarendon Press, 1945.

———. "The Life of Boswell." *Yale Review* 35 (1946): 445–60.

———. "Boswell Revalued." In *Literary Views,* edited by Carroll Camden. Chicago: University of Chicago Press, 1964.

———. "Boswell's University Education." In *Johnson, Boswell and Their Circle: Essays Presented to L. F. Powell.* Oxford: Clarendon Press, 1965.

———. *James Boswell: The Earlier Years, 1740–1769.* New York: McGraw-Hill, 1966.

Poulet, Georges. *The Metamorphoses of the Circle.* Translated by Carley Dawson and Elliott Coleman. Baltimore: Johns Hopkins Press, 1966.

Price, Martin. *To The Palace of Wisdom: Studies in Order and Energy from Dryden to Blake.* New York: Doubleday & Co., 1964.

———. "The Other Self: Thoughts about Character in the Novel." In *Imagined Worlds: Essays in Honour of John Butt,* edited by Maynard Mack and Ian Gregor. London: Methuen & Co., 1968.

Rader, Ralph W. "Literary Form in Factual Narrative: The Example of Boswell's *Johnson.*" In *Essays in Eighteenth-Century Biography,* edited by Philip B. Daghlian. Bloomington: Indiana University Press, 1968.

Scott, Geoffrey. "The Making of The *Life of Johnson,*" Vol. 6 of *Private Papers of James Boswell from Malahide Castle in the Collection of*

Lt.-Colonel Ralph Heyward Isham. Mount Vernon, New York: privately printed, 1929.

Sheldon, Esther K. "Boswell's English in the *London Journal*." *PMLA* 62 (1956): 1067–93.

Sherburn, George. "Writing to the Moment: One Aspect." In *Restoration and Eighteenth-Century Literature: Essays in Honor of Alan Dugald McKillop*. Chicago: University of Chicago Press, 1963.

Smollett, Tobias. *Collected Works*. Edited by George Saintsbury. 12 vols. London: Gibbings; Philadelphia: J. Lippincott, 1895–1900.

Spittal, J. K., ed. *Contemporary Criticisms of Dr. Samuel Johnson, His Works, and His Biographers*. London: J. Murray, 1923.

Stauffer, Donald A. *English Biography before 1700*. Cambridge: Harvard University Press, 1930.

———. *The Art of Biography in Eighteenth-Century England*. Princeton: Princeton University Press, 1941.

Sterne, Laurence. *Tristram Shandy*. Edited by James A. Work. New York: Odyssey Press, 1940.

Sutherland, James. "Some Aspects of Eighteenth-Century Prose." In *Essays on the Eighteenth Century Presented to D. Nichol Smith*. Oxford: Clarendon Press, 1945.

———. *On English Prose*. Toronto: University of Toronto Press, 1957.

Tillinghast, A. J. "Boswell Playing a Part." *Renaissance and Modern Studies* 9 (1965): 86–97.

———. "The Moral and Philosophical Basis of Johnson's and Boswell's Idea of Biography." In *Johnsonian Studies*, edited by Magdi Wahba. Cairo: Société Orientale de Publicité, 1962.

Tinker, Chauncey Brewster. *Young Boswell*. Boston and London: Atlantic Monthly Press, 1922.

Toulmin, Stephen, and June Goodfield. *The Discovery of Time*. New York: Harper & Row, 1965. Reprinted as Harper Torchbook, New York, 1966.

Van Ghent, Dorothy. *The English Novel: Form and Function*. New York: Rinehart & Company, 1953. Reprinted as Harper Torchbook, New York, 1961.

Warton, Thomas. *Observations on The Faerie Queene of Spenser* [1754, 2d ed. 1762]. London: printed by C. Stower, for R. Dutton, 1807.

Wellek, René. *The Rise of English Literary History*. Chapel Hill: University of North Carolina Press, 1941.

———. "Concepts of Form and Structure in Twentieth-Century Criticism." In *Concepts of Criticism*, edited by Stephen G. Nichols, Jr. New Haven: Yale University Press, 1963. Reprint of article in *Neophilologus* 42 (1958): 1–11.

Wimsatt, William K., Jr., and Cleanth Brooks. *Literary Criticism: A Short History*. New York: Alfred A. Knopf, 1957.

Wimsatt, William K., Jr. *The Prose Style of Samuel Johnson*. New Haven: Yale University Press, 1941. Reprinted as Yale Paperback, 1963.

————. *The Verbal Icon: Studies in the Meaning of Poetry.* Lexington: University of Kentucky Press, 1954.

————. "The Fact Imagined: James Boswell." In *Hateful Contraries.* Lexington: University of Kentucky Press, 1965.

Wolcot, John [Peter Pindar]. *A Poetical and Congratulatory Epistle to James Boswell, Esq. on His Journal of a Tour to the Hebrides with the Celebrated Dr. Johnson.* London, 1786.

à Wood, Anthony. *Athenae Oxonienses* [1691–1692]. Edited, with additions, and a continuation by Philip Bliss. 4 vols. London: printed for F. C. & J. Rivington, 1813–1820.

Yates, Frances A. *The Art of Memory.* Chicago: University of Chicago Press, 1966.

INDEX

Addison, Joseph, 92, 93, 97, 100, 120, 121; influence on JB's style, 28, 49; "On the Pleasures of the Imagination," 41–42; quoted, 42n
Auchinleck, Alexander Boswell, Lord, 65

Bailey, Margery, 102
Barber, Francis, 13, 18, 50
Beardsley, Monroe: on literary form and structure, 44n, 52n, 57; quoted, 52n
Beauclerk, Topham, 9
Blair, Hugh, 93, 94, 98; general influence on JB, 117–21, 125
Boswell, James: compares biographers to portrait painters, 1; melancholia of, 2–3, 25, 73–74, 81, 124–25, 126; on biography, 3–5; on Hawkins, 5; likes various views of SJ, 14, 50; sees SJ as complex yet static, 14–15, 32–33, 51, 126; mystery as a stimulus to, 14–15, 125–26; fears loss of individuality, 21–22, 67–70; fragmented identity of, 21–22, 70–72, 75–76; and Hume, 22; and *The Scots Magazine*, 25; disagrees with SJ, 27; and Addison, 28, 41; and *Rasselas*, 28,

56–57; memory of, 43–44, 114, 125n; ambivalence about introspection, 61–62; and John Reid affair, 64–67; compares himself to Burke, 65; egotism and self-consciousness of, 67–70; drafts Inviolable Plan, 68, 107; projected works of, 69n; ability to melt into a crowd, 70; models for behavior, 70; and *The London Magazine*, 70; fears death, 74, 81; and the theater, 75; theatrical personality of, 75; and Louisa, 75, 80, 97; on Goldsmith, 76–77; basis of friendship with SJ, 81; sees friendship with SJ as static, 82; wife's antagonism to SJ, 90; prose style of, 91–123 passim; and Andrew Erskine, 95; periodic sentences in writings of, 112, 114, 123; shorthand method of, 114–16; and Adam Smith, 117, 121; and Hugh Blair, 117–21, 125; spatializes the past and the mind, 132–34, 136–37; imagery in the writings of, 135n
Account of Corsica, An, 26n, 88–89
Hypochondriack, The, 94, 98, 99,

161